GW01003240

To
Have and
to Hold

To Have and to Hold

The Feminine
Mystique at Work
in a Happy Marriage

JILL RENICH

ZONDERVAN PUBLISHING HOUSE

OF THE ZONDERVAN CORPORATION
GRAND RAPIDS, MICHIGAN 49506

To Have and to Hold

© 1972 by The Zondervan Corporation, Grand Rapids, Mich.

Library of Congress Catalog Card Number 74-171203

Seventeenth printing   1978
ISBN 0-310-31812-2

Printed in the United States of America

To
My Beloved
Fred

Contents

Acknowledgments

It is hard to express the deep appreciation I feel for the contributions of many people without whose dedicated help this book could never have been written.

To my parents, Dr. and Mrs. R. A. Torrey, Jr., whose careful training, high ideals and fine example kept me encouraged.

A special tribute is due to my husband, Fred, whose patience and forgiving love is still teaching me, after twenty-seven years, how to be a loving wife and mother.

This book could never have been written if it were not for the cooperation of all our children: Jan, Rose, Rick and Lyn and two young ladies, Phyllis and Peggy, who made their home with us.

To Jean Sudyk who has prodded me on for three years with her encouragement and suggestions as she read and helped revise the manuscript.

To Peggy Thompson who not only typed and retyped parts of the book, but gave a month of her summer to do the final draft.

I am indebted to Blanche Miller for her understanding concern which helped to get this message out.

An expression of thanks and gratitude is due to my typist, Orpha Erickson, to Barbara Brown, Betty Bogart and Kay VanAllen who also contributed to typing or retyping various chapters, and to my neighbor, Kathy Surfus, who gave helpful insights.

I am indebted to the scores of women who are my friends and have taught me many lessons and contributed to the stories (identifying factors were changed) which I trust will help many a woman to be a better wife . . .

"WHOSE PRICE IS FAR ABOVE RUBIES"

Why I Wrote This Book

Many confusing contemporary philosophies are contributing to the disintegration of marriage and family living. The point and purpose for a happy home have been lost. Young people are confused and older people are searching. Many are looking with hope to those who have found the way into a satisfying, solid and harmonious married life. God, who designed marriage for companionship and purposeful living, has also given many instructions and illustrations in the Bible for the "how to." As we go into our study for a happy marriage, we will build around these principles.

Many books on marriage are more helpful if read by both husband and wife. This one is more helpful if read *only* by the wife. However, many of the principles used in this book apply to any situation where people live and work together.

Deep within each person is the basic knowledge of right and wrong. But only God can give the insight into our behavior and the *power* through redemption in Jesus Christ *to do* what we know *we ought to do*. Dealings with God and changes in attitude are deeply personal matters. Many life-changing choices are made alone with God.

Using your Bible and a notebook, answer honestly the questions asked throughout this book. This can help you to find your own God-given answers to a life style within the framework of your marriage and family.

To Have . . . and to Hold is a book which could be used as a study guide for young people before marriage or for newlyweds to awaken them to the realization of what marriage is all about and to help them set ideals and goals toward which they may work.

Pastors, church workers and concerned women will find this a helpful book to lend or give to troubled women who share their problems and come for help. Many women find it easier to accept the ideas of a woman with whom they can identify.

Mothers will find help here to guide their daughters into a happy marriage. What a joy it has been to share these principles with our eldest daughter, Jan, who is now the happy wife of her wonderful husband, Bob.

Why did I write this book? Because I believe each wife has all the potential and God-given help needed to grow into the wife that encourages the highest and best in *her* husband.

Eight Suggestions to Make This Book More Valuable to You

1. Read each chapter twice before going on to the next one.

2. As you read, ask yourself if you can apply any of the suggestions.

3. Ask God to show you the principles that could apply to your life and situation.

4. Underline important ideas.

5. Keep a notebook to write down the ideas which would be helpful in your marriage.

6. Study and answer the questions at the end of each chapter and review your answers periodically.

7. Most important of all, remember to thank God with all your heart for each evidence of progress you see.

8. Plan to share your progress with women around you who also may be looking for answers.

"What He does for you He can do for others."

Part One:

Understanding Your Husband

1
Looking at Marriage

"Hi, darling. I'm home," Jim called as he stamped through the back door.

"Oh, Jim, I'm so glad you weren't late tonight. Dinner is nearly ready. I've done the chops in a casserole just like the ones you enjoyed so much at Jeannie's the other night. It takes a lot longer, but they sure taste better than just plain fried."

"Great, I'm starved! It's getting colder out. That snow will be glazed with ice by morning."

After supper, the kitchen tidied, Jim lounged in his favorite chair, buried in the paper. Nancy sank down on the sofa with a sigh of fatigue after a full, busy day. The restful quiet was shattered by the doorbell. Jim looked up questioningly as Nancy hurried to answer it.

"Why, it's Mr. and Mrs. Wells," she announced happily. Looking over Nancy's shoulder, Jim's eager expectancy changed to controlled displeasure as he saw the snow glistening on the porch and Mrs. Wells clinging to the railing as she cautiously climbed the slippery steps.

Nancy's heart sank as she remembered Jim's hurried, "Sweetheart, can you sweep the steps today? I just don't have time," as he kissed her goodby this morning. She meant to . . . how could she have forgotten?

There was always something — something she forgot, or didn't get around to, or just couldn't manage, and Jim always noticed and was unhappy. How could she. . . . She pushed her thoughts aside and smiled a warm greeting to their friends. The evening went well, and even Jim enjoyed the guests after trying to make light of the slippery steps.

When the Wells had gone, Jim flared, "How in the world can I keep my mind on my job when I have to supervise the home, too?"

"I can't remember everything," Nancy defended herself. "The house was clean, anyway."

After a few words, Jim clammed up. Nancy's housekeeping was enough to drive any man out of his mind. If she really cared. . . .

It was not really Nancy's housekeeping that disturbed him, but the neglect of little areas. It was true the house was usually clean, but the buffet and the top of the piano were always a collecting place for the family junk . . . and the dangerous, icy steps — that was unforgiveable!

Jim is unfair. He makes mountains out of molehills. I am a good mother. I keep the house clean and cook good meals. Why should he make so much fuss over every little thing I forget, Nancy complained bitterly to herself.

They went to bed in the thick, uncomfortable silence of personal hurt.

* * * * *

Nancy and Jim had entered marriage with high ideals. Their home was going to be different; but, like many couples, they did not know how to translate their ideals into a working reality.

- How do you make your ideals work?
  - How do you communicate with a man who sees things so differently than you?
    - How can you understand the reasoning of one who has such a different viewpoint?
    - How do you handle differences creatively?
      - How do you transform hurt into love?

How do you keep love ever growing and inspire those heart-warming words,

"Darling, you're wonderful!"

There is no doubt Nancy and Jim love each other, but the incident of the snowy steps reveals the lack of one very vital ingredient in their relationship. Each wrapped in his own personal hurt, failed to communicate to the other the understanding needed to resolve their quarrel.

It takes time to learn how to put oneself in the other person's place — to see with his eyes, from his perspective. Jim, seeing the hazard of the slippery steps, became fearful of the consequences should Mrs. Wells fall. On top of that, his pride was threatened for what he felt to be negligent housekeeping. Also he may have felt somewhat guilty for not having taken care of the steps himself, instead of asking Nancy.

Had Nancy taken a minute to think how Jim felt, rather than taking the accusation so personally, she might have answered with the real sincerity and understanding which could have changed the picture to —

"I'm sorry, Jim. I should have swept the steps when you asked me. I shouldn't have forgotten, but I was so busy all day and got so excited about trying to make those chops, I forgot. I'm thankful no one fell."

"Yeah, good thing we have a railing, and the chops *were* good. I should have thought to sweep the steps myself while you put the kids to bed."

"Oh, no, I should have done it before you came home. You shouldn't have to worry about home, too, after your day at the office."

"Oh, darling, you're wonderful," and in Jim's heart he would think how lucky he was to have such an understanding wife. . . . *How many wives understand how a man feels after a gruelling day at the office? Nancy usually looked lovely when he came home. She*

19

never failed to greet him eagerly — he was a pretty lucky fellow.

Most couples enter into marriage idealistically. Each eagerly anticipates, from their love for one another, living "happily ever after." But how well-prepared are you for the responsibilities and privileges of marriage? Many years are given to training for success in one's life vocation. However, one's vocation can be changed if unsatisfactory. It also ends at retirement — but marriage . . . *that* vocation is for *life!*

Yet how much time is spent in conscious preparation for marriage? You tell me: How much time have you spent preparing to make your marriage a success? Have you made a study of basic differences between men and women and how they are expressed? Do you know the most important ingredients to insure a happy and successful marriage?

Before I married, it never occurred to me to read a book on how to be a good wife, although with all my heart I wanted to be one. As a young couple, we were counseled to read a book on sex, but no one suggested a book on being an adequate wife. In my heart, I felt there were certain attitudes a woman should have toward her husband, her home, and her children, but they were rather hazy.

In the early years of our marriage, while Fred and I were seeking to make our marriage all it should be, I looked around and began to wonder if there were couples — apart from my own father and mother — who had worked out an ideal marriage. Then God graciously led us to stay in a home in Australia which proved to be a real blessing to me. The ideals lived out by that wife have influenced and guided me through the years.

An Australian Couple

My husband was holding special inter-church meetings in a little Australian town. The Methodist minister's wife invited us to stay in their home.

Our little daughter, Jan, had been left in Brisbane, because we knew a child would be an added burden.

As we entered this home, we immediately sensed something different. The house was neat and clean. There was an atmosphere of love and freedom. Our hostess received us with genuine warmth as she served tea, but without "fussing" over us. We felt welcome even though we knew our presence was a great inconvenience. Their eldest daughter, who was through school, taught music at home and helped her mother around the house. We had a lovely time talking, and soon the other children came tumbling in from school — three more girls and a boy, the youngest. The children seemed happy to have us and then enthusiastically shared with their mother the events of their day.

The father was away on a trip, but the attitude of the whole family toward him and their eager anticipation of his return made me most anxious to meet him. When the family found we had left our little daughter behind, they insisted I return to Brisbane and bring her back.

On the second day I began to trail the wife as she did her laundry and cooked the meals. The housework took a great deal of time, because the living conditions were difficult. She laughed about not being able to sit down and talk, but was glad to talk to me as she went happily about her work. She told me of the women who came to her with burdened hearts and of her opportunities to share with them the power of God as she had experienced it. There had been many a prayer meeting around the kitchen table as she paused in her household duties to commend a troubled woman to her God, who not only heard but also answered her prayers. Her eyes filled with love when she talked about her husband and his anticipated return.

I showered this woman with questions about her marriage. How I thank God for her openness with me and her willingness to share the rich experiences of years while my own hopes and dreams were still somewhat nebulous.

Mrs. Baxter (I'll call her) met her husband at school. Both were active Christians and took seriously the responsibilities of marriage and a life dedicated to service for others. She had a deep compassion for women in need and had become an able speaker. In talking through their life goals, the Baxters decided that her abilities as well as his should be used in their life work. While the children were young and the physical work was demanding, he shared in the work of the home, which enabled her to help him in his work. As the children grew older, they were carefully trained to take over their share of the home responsibilities.

In the morning Mr. Baxter rose first and brought his wife a cup of tea. Afterward she would waken each of the five children, and for half an hour each member of the family had his own time alone with God for prayer and Bible reading. Then the children would dress and hurry about their assigned tasks. Comfortable orderliness enabled the children to leave for school without pressure.

As I talked with Mrs. Baxter, I could see her devotion to her husband. *His* need was her first concern. The children idolized their father and felt that he must not be hindered in the effectiveness of his ministry. The whole community reflected the attitude of deep respect his family had for him.

One day, as Mrs. Baxter was talking about her husband, she said, "One word from the children's father means more than ten from me."

"That's right," laughed a daughter who was standing nearby. But I saw it was the mother who had created this attitude of respect for her husband and his few words.

I saw demonstrated by Mrs. Baxter that a woman with strength of character and the freedom of self-acceptance can channel her strength behind her husband without losing her own individuality. This was no mousy woman riding on her husband's coattails. Here was a capable, godly woman who had much to contribute to her husband and children as well as to her community.

Principles for a Solid Marriage

What principles enabled the Baxters to have such an ideally happy marriage? I doubt if the Baxters could have put them into words, but I saw they had built their lives on the foundation that *marriage is for life*. Accepting this as the basis for their marriage, they *expected* to work through their differences. They worked toward a merging of their two lives so they could effectively contribute to their generation.

First of all, Mrs. Baxter's *attitude toward her husband* was one of love, which revealed itself in acceptance, respect, support, openness and cooperative sharing without competition.

Second, Mrs. Baxter's *attitude toward herself* was one of self-acceptance. She had a sense of purpose in her life and marriage. She was creative and industrious in the management of their home and the children, whom she carefully trained in helpfulness and character.

Third, Mrs. Baxter's *attitude toward her circumstances* was one of happy acceptance. She was cheerful about their limited budget, her heavy work load and the need to stay home while the children were young. She sought opportunities to be useful within the framework of her home. Her busy mind was always mulling over creative ways to benefit herself and her family. In summary, the following seemed to be the guilding principles for the Baxters:

- There was mutual respect and acceptance between them.
- They talked over and planned goals for their marriage.

23

- They discussed each other's strengths and found what each could contribute toward their life purpose.

- They planned as realistically as possible to merge their talents.

- They kept the lines of communication open, so that as situations changed they could find a new course of action that was mutually agreeable.

DON'T STOP READING YET!

I know this seems idealistic and you're thinking, "That's fine, if you have *her* husband, but mine . . . !

- He never talks.
  - I don't know what he thinks.
    - We never even thought of motives and goals. We just got married."

Stay with me. Somewhere in this book you may find the key or several keys to unlock a whole new world of happiness in your marriage. These thoughts are for those on the edge of formulating ideals and getting off to a good start as well as for those who find themselves (shall I be really blunt and say?) in a mess.

Just a word of encouragement before I go on. Remember, all of us have problems. There is nothing wrong with having a problem, but it is wrong not to try to find the answer. There *is* an answer to your problem. Instant cures are rare, although I have seen and experienced a few. It usually takes time and effort to find the root of the difficulty:

- To unravel and change deep-seated attitudes
- To understand and forgive from the heart
- To build a harmonious relationship
- To love and be loved.

But it *can be done*. I've seen it happen!

24

An Ideal Spelled Out

Let's start with an ideal. Then we can work out clear, definite steps for becoming the wife who will hear more often the words,

"Darling, you're wonderful!"

A man of great wisdom once asked this question: "A worthy woman who can find? For her price is far above rubies."

Why should this woman be so hard to find? What makes a priceless woman? This same man of wisdom — a husband — answers his own question by setting out clearly some qualities of character which describe this "gem."

- Her husband can *safely* trust her.
- She is a woman of faith and joy.
- She is wise and compassionate.
- She keeps herself well physically.
- She faces life realistically.
- Her home and family are thoughtfully cared for.
- She gets up early and organizes each day.
- She takes time for long-range planning.
- She is industrious and shows good judgment in business matters.
- She spends their income wisely and works hard.
- Her whole life is an asset to her husband.
- Her children love and deeply respect her.
- Her husband is proud of her.

Read Proverbs 31:10-31. Solomon portrays a complete wife with feminine qualities and divine virtues — a woman of integrity, emotionally stable and loving. She is a capable homemaker, concerned for others, spiritually mature, inner-directed, and flexible, a "priceless" wife!

This standard may seem overwhelming. You feel you

could never be all this; or you may say, "I'm doing pretty well — who needs it?"

You're Needed

My first purpose in writing this book is to give guidelines for those who are anticipating marriage. Next I'd like to offer hope to the discouraged wife — and for those with a good marriage, a challenge to an even better one! For you who are happily married, perhaps I can help you find words with which to share the principles which contributed to *your* rich life. Then, as you share your experiences, many more women will profit by them.

Chapter One

Looking at Marriage

Questions to Ask Yourself

In your notebook write down the questions and list the qualities you think make an ideal wife. Remember, it will take time to formulate life principles and find what you feel to be a worthy life style for your marriage.

— Do you agree with the ideal that "marriage is for life"?
— If so, what steps can you take to assure its permanence? If not, what will happen to your marriage?
— What should be included in your role as a wife . . . your rights, his rights to your time, division of labor, social life, handling of money, etc.?
— What is your attitude to homemaking or your purpose in following a career?
— What are worthwhile goals for your marriage?
— How can your family contribute to the needs of the world today?
— Is your husband a better man for having married you? How?

2
The Importance of Right Attitudes

All of us anticipate two things from marriage: happiness and success.

Since each of us is different, your idea of success may differ from mine. But there is one common requirement in every successful marriage: *We have to get along with a person!*

Your idea of happiness may be different from mine, but real happiness comes from within and cannot be completely dependent upon circumstances or another person. Although your concept of an ideal wife and your husband's concept may differ, your happiness in marriage will depend on three basic attitudes:

- your attitude toward your husband
  - your attitude toward yourself
    - your attitude toward your circumstances

If your attitudes are wrong they will distort reality and twist your relationship.

Faulty concepts of marriage provide a weak foundation for a home.

Right attitudes, followed by right actions, are the basis for a strong foundation in a happy marriage.

Kathy's Attitude

"What has made your husband so ambitious?" I asked Kathy.

"I really don't know," Kathy answered simply. "When I married John he was shoveling coal, but I loved him and as long as he was happy in what he was doing I didn't care what it was. I don't know what made the change, but he went back and finished high school, and now he is taking night courses at the university. He has changed jobs six times but now has a good office job with a large company."

"Did you push him to go to school or to get a better job?"

"No, I didn't. I believe John has so much ability he could do really well in anything he likes, and it makes no difference to me what John does, just so he is happy doing it. He's the breadwinner and I feel a man does best when he is happy in his work. When he thought about going to college and worried about how long it would take him to get a degree, I said, 'So what if it takes you until you're forty! By then there would be even more opportunities in the work you enjoy. What difference does it make how long it takes? At least when you are through you have something.'"

"But it takes a lot of money to go to school, besides having John away evenings," I commented.

"Yes, it does cost money, but John loves the challenge of his studies, so I'm glad he can do it. God supplies our needs and sometimes in the most unexpected ways, so I don't worry."

Acceptance

Kathy has discovered the first principle for a happy marriage — acceptance. John is accepted as he is and not as she wishes he were. Kathy is not *trying* to change John, but in this freedom John is inspired by her love and confidence.

"I don't agree with Kathy," you may say. "I think it is my *duty* to help my husband change. It's for his own good. After all, it's my duty as a wife to help him, and how can I help him if I don't work toward making him a better person?"

On the surface this seems to be a commendable idea, but is it? Let's think. Suppose your husband wanted to change *you*. How would you feel? Accepted? Accepted

28

for alterations? Not really accepted or appreciated? Then, as your feeling of non-acceptance and inadequacy grows, distrust and tension could begin to build.

Concentrating on changing a man's character can't help but put the wife in a superior position. This would accentuate differences and/or supposed weaknesses in the husband. Would this not eventually destroy love, confidence and communication?

Acceptance, full acceptance, sets a man free — free to be his best without your pushing or nagging. This acceptance gives a man the confidence he needs in his work. He is free to face the workaday world and its challenges. Acceptance builds and strengthens personal confidence which in turn will make a man far more adequate in his role as a responsible, loving husband.

Non-Acceptance

Some women unwittingly make their husbands feel unacceptable as they are. Sometimes a man feels that money or status is more important to his wife than he is. This puts him under much pressure.

> Jane did this. She came from a professional family and found she could not accept George's abilities. Status was vitally important to her, so she pushed him up the "ladder of success." Under the pressure of added responsibilities, George became more and more tense. Jane, intent on her goal, didn't even notice.
>
> Finally, desperate from the mounting pressure, George could take no more and walked out on everything. Months passed without a word from George, and the heartbroken and humiliated Jane was forced to move in with her parents.
>
> George wandered aimlessly for years before coming to grips with his problem. In time he was able to return to his wife and family, and together he and Jane sought professional help for their marriage. Jane had to face the fact that George

29

simply was not cut out to be an executive. It was hard, too, for her to accept a different standard of living. But, because she truly loved her husband, she began to accept him as he was, rather than as she had hoped he would be. Their marriage was saved. They were able to build on the solid rock of reality, rather than on the illusion of unrealistic dreams.

Don't be afraid to encourage your husband and love him as he is. Let your faith in him be the mirror in which he can come to see God's best for him.

Very often a man is under such pressure at work to improve himself that he needs your faith and confidence in him as a constant source of strength so that he can face the daily grind and the pressures of his job.

Differences

Most women marry an "ideal." There are qualities which have drawn your husband to you, and qualities which have drawn you to him. The first aura of love and emotion blinds you and you do not consider how differently you may react later to that which appeals to you now. Perhaps your vivacious personality will wear a bit thin as you rattle on and on when he wants quiet after talking to people at work all day. . . . The depth of character which his quietness implies becomes irritating, especially if you've been alone all day and you begin to think he's moody or indifferent. Or it could be the other way around, he thinks you're too quiet or moody.

You may wonder. *Why* is Bob so careless with money? But you loved it when he spent his money so freely on you before marriage! You loved his easygoing way then. He had a quieting effect on you when you tended to be high-strung. But now . . . How do you get a lazy man out of bed in the morning? You begin to fret, inwardly. How can you accept *this* man with these traits of character?

30

Accepting Differences

The time for creativity in adjusting to marriage comes when personality differences create conflict. Then you really need to do some *constructive* thinking. When these serious differences arise between you, you will probably react in one of three ways:

1. You no longer see any good in your husband.
2. You close your eyes to his faults and insist he's perfect.
3. You accept him as he is, seeing his "different- ness" as a complement to your personality.

The third way is the basis for harmony in your marriage.

Many problems of adjustment come from differences in temperament. God created each of us differently in order that we may supplement and strengthen each other — not clash. In thinking through your differences, remember that they are not "good" or "bad" in them- selves. Your husband's easy-going way is not neces- sarily laziness just because you are a ball of fire. If you were alike, your home might explode! God made the two of you different because He had a different sphere of usefulness for each of you in your marriage. You are to complement, supplement and strengthen each other through these differences. As there is infinite variety in the temperaments of people, so there are infi- nite ways of combining your differences for effective living. Remember, God did not intend for a race horse to pull a plow! Choose to accept your husband as God has made him, without judging him.

Rather than falling under the weight of what you feel to be his "weakness" and clashing with what you feel to be his "wrong way," remind yourself that he sees with different eyes. Your husband can safely trust you when he knows you have accepted him as he is.

No two people work in quite the same way. Believe it or not, some men can work in a clutter and really get a lot done. Some men are night owls, others are early birds. Some men work best under pressure with many irons in the fire; others are content with one job and their home. Some men love to be out just about every night in the week, while others never want a social evening.

What if your husband's way is the exact opposite of yours? What if you can't find anything on his cluttered work bench? That is his domain. Set him free. Let him be himself and function in the way which is comfortable for him.

"How can I accept my husband as he is when he cares nothing about the house and won't keep things repaired? Our bankbook never balances, either. How can I accept this?"

That's a good question. But remember, he sees things from a different perspective. As you want your husband to accept the fact that you are a good cook and not quite so good about ironing, so you need to accept the fact that he may be very handy at mechanics, but not very good at figures. As you love cooking but hate ironing, so he may hate house repairs. After prayer for wisdom, you and your husband can talk over together how the home needs can be best met. Pool your insights and seek to harmonize your viewpoints. Perhaps you should take over the accounts if accounting is one of your strong points. Why insist that he do it just because you think this is the job for the "head of the home"? If neither you nor your husband are good "fixers," perhaps you should rearrange your budget and hire a carpenter!

Each situation is different and each couple has a different combination of gifts and ideas. No problem is resolved by nagging, running away, or refusing to face it. But when you discover you can't agree on the solution to a problem after discussing it quite thoroughly, *drop it for a time*. When you keep on and on, your emotions become involved, and it becomes difficult to think clearly. Sometimes in the heat of an argument you hurl accusations which can leave scars for life. Then you lose sight of the ideas you are trying to share.

Pray about it together (or alone if your husband prefers), looking to God for His way. He understands you both and knows the best solution for your problem. Trust God. *Expect* Him to show you the answer. It may not be what *you* thought it should be. Incidentally, you'll be learning patience too, as you are waiting expectantly to find God's way.

Don't be afraid of differences. In marriage certain differences may exist happily side by side. Handled wisely, they can be healthy and challenging. A woman sometimes talks off the top of her head. This can be trying to a logically minded husband. But brainstorming for new ideas is done this way. Let your husband sort out with you workable solutions to your differences, because, when your ideas are challenged, you have the opportunity to think through your conclusions more carefully. They may be valid!

A wife who tries to justify wrong attitudes or poor judgment loses her own self-respect and her husband's respect as well. You will be amazed how much more your husband will love you and trust you if you admit it when you are wrong and try to change.

In the early days of our marriage we had some rather "warm" discussions. When we came to an impasse, we learned to drop the subject. When we'd bring up the matter later, it often amazed me to find, for some unknown reason, that we then agreed! The emotional heat of an argument can disintegrate communication.

Ask God to enable you to communicate acceptance with love and understanding. Love stimulates a desire and a willingness to see the other person's point of view, to be objective, and, if you disagree, to do it graciously. "I'm listening to you" shows you care enough to try to remedy the problem. There is a difference between *listening* to what others are saying and merely *hearing* words.

Understanding

Next to acceptance, the most important key to a happy marriage is understanding. Understanding your husband should be one of your most important concerns. Does he feel you really understand him? Here are some questions to check your U.Q. (understanding quotient). Can you answer them?

1. What is the happiest thing that ever happened to your husband? What brings him the most happiness today?

2. What about you does he appreciate the most?

3. What has been the hardest experience in his life, the saddest thing that ever happened to him? What causes him the most anxiety today? What are his deep fears?

4. What are his secret ambitions, his goals for his life?

5. On what does he place the most value? What is his attitude toward money, savings, insurance and security?

6. What is his attitude toward sex, children, his family? Your family?

7. What man or men does he most admire?

8. What traits of yours would he like to see changed?

Do you really know and understand your husband? Can he talk to you and not be ridiculed? Can he confide in you and know his confidences will be safely guarded? Do you minimize his weaknesses and emphasize his manliness and his strength? Do you create a climate in which he feels safe to voice his fears because you believe in him?

Work Load

When a man marries, he very matter-of-factly sets aside, in the name of love, his freedom and contracts to take on the full social and economic responsibility for his wife and children. He must remember each day that on the success or failure of his efforts rest the happiness, health and well-being of his family.

Are you close enough to your husband to know how heavily, at times, this burden weighs upon him? A good wife can do much to lighten her husband's load by showing she understands and appreciates the magnitude of his life commitment. Most men do not talk about these things with their wives or children. They carry the burden alone, facing a highly competitive world — a world too often filled with injustice and inequity.

Some wives compare their husbands with other men. They nag, "Look at all the money Bill makes," or "I wish you had banker's hours like Ed has," or "Why can't you get ahead or insist on a raise?" When Jim took a part-time job to make more money, Lil fussed because he was never home. When Beth's husband tried to change his hours to please her, she complained he wasn't making enough money. . . .

Your husband cannot be compared to another man. God has created no one else like him. God wants you to understand him — his strengths, his weaknesses, temperament, likes, dislikes and abilities. Is your husband happy in his work? Does it challenge him? Does he have to work long hours with a low salary? Is he often home late because he is carrying heavy responsibilities in his work? Do you see his job as *he does* and understand how *he feels*? Can you accept his long hours just so he is happy? Can you communicate your understanding?

Tom found his work hard and challenging but often discouraging. At times he wondered if he could handle his difficult assignments. Never would he admit to his wife that he couldn't do his job, but he often discussed his work with her. "You can do it," she assured him. Her quiet faith in his ability lifted his spirits and gave him the renewed confidence he needed as he returned to his work.

After Work

It is difficult for a man to make the transition from the competition of his job to the demands of his home. Often, a man's irritability, his self-absorption, his unreasonable demands on his wife are only expressions of his reaction to the hard and anxious struggle of the day. His bragging, carelessness about the house, indifference toward her and the children are often the outlets for the tensions of the day. Think of this and prepare yourself while he is at work so you won't snap back. Anticipate his behavior and ask God to give you His love and gentleness which is the balm your husband needs. Your support, admiration and encouragement will strengthen him and make his burden lighter, his worries less acute.

Do you understand how *your* husband's need can best be met? Some men want supper immediately; others need a half-hour to unwind. Some want to read the paper or play with the children; some want to watch the news on TV or just chat with their wives, sharing the day's difficulties or successes.

Ralph returned home from work any time between four-thirty and six o'clock. Mary planned meals which would free her to sit down whenever Ralph arrived so they could enjoy a cup of coffee together. This helped him to make the transition from the office to his home. Sometimes Ralph talked and shared his day. Other times he was quiet. Mary tried to sense his need and meet it — she knew talking was not necessary for them to

36

communicate. After coffee, as Ralph relaxed over the evening paper, Mary put the finishing touches on dinner.

Few men are even aware of this transition problem. Unless you can identify and meet your husband's need, the transition may come from a stop for a drink on the way home. There, in the undemanding atmosphere of the bar, he can adjust to his change of world's — from the "marketplace" to his home.

Approval

A friend, whose husband I scarcely knew, often told me what a wonderful husband she had. Over a long period of time the story unfolded. In his youth the husband had been in trouble with the law. He was rough and crude in his ways. There were times when he'd yell at the children. One son was much like the father had been in his youth. Out of concern, the father treated his son so severely that the boy began to develop serious problems. The wife told me how her husband loved his family and how they worked together as a unit on different projects, such as making things for Christmas, or decorating the house for a child's birthday party. The children were not pushed aside but included in things the father did around the home. His wife *believed* in him, saw his potential, *accepted* him and *showed* her approval. As a result of the wife's positive attitude, the atmosphere in their home is happier. Friends who knew this husband before he married, marvel at the change in him. There are still rough spots because of the lack of spiritual harmony. "But that will come," his wife tells me happily. "I just have to learn patience."

Approval is a magic key. You can't approve of everything, but do you emphasize the things you can approve? Many wives are so busy looking at areas that *need* improvement and figuring out a way to improve them that they haven't time to appreciate qualities that merit praise.

Acceptance is a primary basis for increasing your husband's potential. Approval frees a man to work out his potential. There is always something you can approve. Much depends on how you look at things. You know how a negative person often brings out the worst in you, but a person who gives you the feeling he approves of you (whether it is your husband or a friend) gives you just the boost you need to do your best. God will show you areas you can approve. Ask Him. Look for one thing and you will be surprised how you begin to see others.

Appreciation

How is your "appreciation quotient"? Did you show the appreciation you felt for what your husband did *or* said the other day? The word appreciate really means "to raise in value." It's the opposite of depreciate, or to lower in value.

> Jerry returned home upset because he had a cut in pay. He dreaded giving his check to his wife. Sherry saw her husband's distress and realized that his self-esteem as a good provider was damaged. She immediately took this opportunity to assure Jerry that *he* and *his happiness* were far more important to her than their income.

Show your husband how much you appreciate him. This cannot but draw out his very best. Stop and think what appreciation does for you. Everyone wants to be appreciated. No one wants to be taken for granted.

> "My wife never expresses any appreciation," a young man said to me wistfully. "I took Maria out for dinner a week ago and she never even thanked me. It takes all the joy out of doing things for her."

Several weeks later, I had a note from Maria. She was concerned about her attitude to Don. "I'm learning to *express my appreciation and show my love*. Don and I are so much happier."

God lets us know He values us and that we are essential to Him. You know how excited you were when this first dawned on you. Nothing He asked you to do was too much.

Before we go any further, stop reading and open your heart in prayer to God. Ask Him to show you all the good things He has built into your husband. God loves your husband and has been working in his life over the years.

Right now, list five things you can appreciate about your husband.

1. _____
2. _____
3. _____
4. _____
5. _____

Has the space run out? Did you think of that unexpected gift? The time he wanted to take you to some special place? The check he *brings home* each week? (Now, never mind what you think is his motive — just be grateful and thank God for each check.) He doesn't complain when dinner is late. He is not personally demanding. He shares the car without question. He leaves you free to develop your own interests. He does help with the dishes and he will take out the rubbish, and, oh, yes, he doesn't mind mowing the lawn. He is honest, provides adequately for the family, loves the children and you.

There is a difference between mere flattery and sincere appreciation. Flattery gratifies a person's vanity. Appreciation and praise are based upon a person's character and deeds. Recognizing what it is that merits praise, you encourage more praiseworthiness.

Now, go one step further: When you see your husband tonight, tell him how much you appreciate him and his abilities. He can't read your mind, so, for example, say, "I'm so thankful for you. I'm proud of you. You work so hard and you are so dependable."

At first you may feel foolish expressing your appreciation in words, but keep trying. He needs to *hear* you express in words what is *in your heart*. If your personality differs from his, your lack of verbal communication may hide your true feelings of appreciation. Maybe you think you are expressing your appreciation to him in many ways, such as baking his favorite pie or keeping a sparkling house. But these actions do not necessarily communicate your true appreciation for him in language he can understand.

Chapter Two

The Importance of Right Attitudes

Questions to Ask Yourself

— What is your attitude toward your husband's place in the structure of your home?

— How can you achieve unity where your husband and you disagree?

— How do your attitudes toward children and their training differ?

— As you consider the differences in your approach to life, how can you come to an understanding?

— How can you better see his problems from *his* viewpoint? Do you understand what he means by what he says?

— Are you communicating your approval, appreciation, understanding and admiration?

— How are you cultivating friendship with your husband?

3
Meeting His Needs

Four Sides of Marriage

A number of years ago I read a story which expressed so well that marriage is more than physical attraction

The story centered around an attractive, socially ambitious woman with much personal magnetism. She set her heart on a handsome young man whom she won and married. At different times through the years of marriage, her social ambitions, coupled with her lack of love for their home and only daughter drained her husband's love for her. Sensing this, the wife gave herself anew to fan the embers of his desire. For a number of years periodic attention coupled with intense sex appeal kept her husband bound to her.

When the couple approached middle age, the wife sensed once again her husband's coolness. She turned on all her charm, but this time she was unable to draw him to herself. Then he asked for a divorce. His wife was shocked. Her husband loved another woman! Later, the wife met the woman who had won her husband's heart. This woman seemed to lack physical attractiveness and sex appeal, nor was she found in "good" social circles. She loved her home and spent much time with her only child. The wife challenged her husband, "What do you see in her?"

The husband fumbled for words. He had not defined to himself the sweet, loving, understanding qualities which satisfied another side of his deeply emotional nature. Groping for an explanation, he mumbled,

"I see, well — I see — the — the — other side of the moon!"

It's *not* easy to define the "other side of the moon." It would be as different for each man as one woman differs from another! Perhaps the biggest challenge for a wife is to satisfy *all* her husband's needs. This is not done overnight! First of all, it takes a creative love, coupled with time and real thought to discover all his needs. Then one must learn *how to meet* them. The exciting payoff for such love is that most women find their own deep needs fulfilled while working unselfishly toward satisfying their husband's.

A wife has a complex role. In other cultures, where a woman was basically a work horse and a producer of offspring, men took additional wives to satisfy their unmet needs. This might be all right, except it created far more problems than it solved!

In our society a wife has the challenge of being all her husband needs. Happily, she is not left to struggle alone. Our God, who created one woman for one man to be a "proper helper" for him (Genesis 2:20, *Living Bible*), will enable her to fulfill her role completely.

Personal needs fall into four main areas: spiritual, mental, sexual and emotional. These areas make excellent checkpoints for a happy marriage. How you develop each area of your life will largely determine the success or failure of your marriage. Your failure in any of these areas can create a source of deep temptation for your husband. It could lead him to seek the company of women who meet these needs in his life.

> Kathy's mother gave her a piece of sound advice when she first married. "Katherine," she said, "if you find one day that your husband is running around, don't go to the other woman or look anywhere else; start looking in your own home and you'll find the reason why."

May the following pages on the four sides of marriage stimulate deeper insights in your own situation, enabling you to meet more fully your husband's needs in all areas of his life. This then will provide the base from which you could help free your husband from temptation and encourage him to reach his own potential.

SIDE ONE: THE SPIRITUAL CHALLENGE

Deep within the heart of each man God has placed a spiritual nature. In many men this God-awareness is buried beneath a facade of indifference and even ridicule. But even such men appreciate a quality of real and relevant spiritual vitality. However, few men show this appreciation in a way a woman would show it. Therefore it is comforting to *know* each man *has* God-given spiritual hunger, even though hidden.

God created man for Himself. He has a *right way* for each person to live within his circumstances. Living within God's spiritual laws brings glory to Him and peace to each person. God demonstrated an effective life by sending His Son, Jesus Christ, into the world to live completely for others, and then to give His life to "save His people from their sin" — from living selfishly.

Today, the principles of *real* Christianity are little understood; its precepts and principles are little practiced. If women understood how to live the Christian life in the home, other areas of life would develop naturally. A strong Christian home, with understanding and unity, *can be developed* through God's creative love when a wife demonstrates her faith by practical Christianity.

The only way you can live effectively is to put your life literally into God's hands. In essence you say to God, in the quietness of your own heart, "I give my life to You. . . . Come into my heart Lord Jesus. . . . Thank You. . . . Direct my life from within. . . . Direct me clearly enough so that I may do Your will. . . ."

"God's ways are not our ways and His thoughts are not our thoughts." There needs to be a recognition of

His divine wisdom and His divine Lordship. You are created for His eternal purposes. His will for you brings inner fulfillment because of His perfect love toward you.

Let me give you an illustration of practical spirituality.

Doreen's Struggle

Doreen attended church faithfully but heard little that helped in her trying home situation. One day she called Linda three times, barely getting her out the door in time to catch the bus for work. *She's just like her dad,* Doreen thought resentfully. Before nagging Linda out to the bus, she had worn out her patience getting Arnold on his way to the office. *What would they do without her?* It was harder than a day's work to get those two to work — on time.

Doreen wearily poured herself a cup of coffee. Her strength returned, but her resentment mounted as she thought of her poky daughter and procrastinating husband. The ironing was waiting. As tired as she was, she had better get to it. Out on the back porch the iron was plugged in to the drop cord above the board. Months ago Arnold had promised to fix an outlet on the wall for the iron, but his good intentions, coupled with his easy-going way, left this job undone, along with dozens of other little things around the house.

Doreen attacked the ironing with added bitterness. The cord fell out of the plug. She shoved it in again, only to have it fall out a few minutes later. With anger mounting, she found a piece of string and tied the two parts together. How could anyone live as a Christian with such an inconsiderate husband and a lazy daughter?

In everything give thanks flashed across her mind. The special speaker at the church had spoken last night on having a thankful spirit in everything. She thought hotly how young and inexperienced the preacher was. What did he know about difficulties? *He's the head of his house, and he can see that his wife does what he wants,* she thought resentfully. How could she organize her work today and get to the meeting on time?

Arnold came home late. He greeted his wife cheerfully —

"How was your day?" he asked.

"All right, I suppose. You're late and we'll never make it to the meeting on time," she complained.

The meal was eaten in the heaviness of her silent disapproval.

Arnold, Doreen and Linda arrived at church after the first hymn. *How can a deacon be so irresponsible as to arrive late for church? It's bad enough to be careless about our home and my feelings, but carelessness about church duties is inexcusable,* Doreen brooded. It was hard to concentrate on the message of the evening.

"In everything give thanks," came the voice of the speaker again. Doreen thrust the thought aside. *That's all right when you have an ideal situation, but that's impossible for me.* Doreen listened dully as the speaker unfolded further God's standard for the Christian.

During the week Doreen was gripped by the thought that there was more to the Christian life than accepting Christ as Savior and letting it go at that. She began to discover that this was only the beginning of:

- *A new concept* of life, all of it lived effectively for God . . .

- *New attitudes* toward people, accepting them as they are . . .

- *A new outlook,* continual thanksgiving in everything . ..

- *A new perspective,* an awareness of God's purposes in her daily life . . .

- *A new way,* living above her circumstances and not being controlled by them.

45

These ideas about God's expectation of the Christian and the Christian's expectation from God for this new life were stimulating for Doreen.

In the weeks that followed, the words from the Bible coupled with the vivid illustrations from the speaker's life and others he knew came back again and again to Doreen as she worked in the silence of her home. After another exasperating ironing day the words returned to haunt her, "In everything give thanks." It flooded over Doreen that God was speaking to *her* and this time she listened. She began to thank God for being able to iron, tied cord and all. She thanked Him for her husband, for her daughter. As she began to thank God, she found the bitterness fading. As the bitterness faded, she was able to think more clearly.

I've made a lot of my own problems. I'm going to quit nagging Linda, she thought. *Then she'll be late to work and lose her job. . . . That will mean she won't have money for Bible school next year . . . But what am I doing to the pattern of Linda's life? Is my attitude really helping her?*

Gradually Doreen began to see that she needed to let Linda go . . . to God, and let her assume responsibility for herself.

And Arnold? What about him? She should set him free, too. Oh, but the consequences; they seemed even more than God could handle!

That evening Linda could sense a difference in her mother. When Arnold was late for supper, Doreen was waiting quietly, mending his shirt. During the meal Doreen shared with the family how God had spoken to her.

"I see how wrong I have been to nag you both and I want to tell you I'm sorry." Arnold and Linda looked at each other. "Linda, you may set your alarm and if you don't get up, that's up to you. I won't be calling you half a dozen times. You're on your own. And Arnold, I shall stop nagging you about getting to work or church on time."

Doreen had faced her fears in changing her way, but she could scarcely believe what happened the next day and the next. Linda got up with her alarm! Arnold was ready for work and church sooner than usual. God took over when she let go. *Why didn't I do this years ago?* she marveled. And why not? No one had ever *communicated* God's way so clearly as the young preacher. At last she saw, with sudden insight, how she had contributed to the very situation she found so distressing.

Holier Than Thou

Nothing turns a man off faster than a volatile woman with a martyr complex who seeks to impress him with her many "sacrificial church activities."

There is a great difference between the woman who *talks about* being a Christian, insisting on all the letter-of-the-law and the woman who demonstrates her faith by inner peace and outward direction.

Husbands have been heard to comment to their friends that they personally are not very religious; "but when my wife prays something happens," they say with quiet pride.

"Prayer changes things," the motto reads. Our Aunt Edith Torrey challenged us unforgettably with: "What things has *your* prayer changed?" Women can do a lot of talking, but the evidence speaks for itself. Is prayer changing your attitude about your problems, difficulties, situations and misunderstandings? When was the last time God answered your specific prayer?

The Impossible Possible

If you are honest with yourself, you know there are things you ought to do. You are conscious of the areas of homemaking you are shirking and of the times you should have a more forgiving spirit. But actually *doing* what you *know* to be right is another thing. At times

47

it seems impossible. Then what? Right at the point of conscious need *ask* God for His power to do what you know is His will. Then thank Him for hearing your prayer and supplying your need. As you start to obey God, you will find that He meets you and enables you to do what you alone could not do.

I'll never forget how angry I was with Fred one morning. He made an inadvertent comment to me as he went out the door. It triggered instant resentment in me. When I attacked the dishes after he left and mulled over what he had said, my resentment grew. For a few minutes it felt good to nurse my bitterness. But before the dishes were finished I saw how wrong my attitude was. I knew I *had to choose against my feelings,* forgive Fred and ask God to forgive me and completely wash away my resentment. I did. Immediately the resentment died. The cleansing was so complete I can't even remember what Fred said!

Have you been guilty of storing up injustices? Is your husband sometimes mystified by your coolness when he returns home? Let your husband return to stored-up love and a joyous welcome instead.

A vital, functioning faith in God is a woman's most valuable attribute. With this attitude toward God, you can find answers to a happier marriage. God puts a high value on the spiritually mature woman who has developed a meek and quiet spirit. Your deep confidence in the *power of God* is rewarded when you find God's way in each area of your marriage.

In preparation for the questions to ask yourself, read Psalm 23, meditating on God's provision for you.

Chapter Three

Spiritual Challenge in Marriage

Questions to Ask Yourself

— In what areas of your life do you find it hard to trust God?

— What are your fears?

— What do you want God to do for you?

— Do you really desire a change?

— Are you secretly preferring your problems to finding an answer?

"Delight yourself also in the Lord, and He will give you the desires and secret petitions of your heart" (Psalm 37:4, *Amplified*).

SIDE TWO: MENTAL STIMULUS

Next to and along with the importance of a spiritually challenging life, it is necessary for a wife to be a mental challenge to her husband.

Much of a husband's contentment comes from the mental stimulus his wife can be to him. Without this, a marriage can easily sink into a rut. Zest for living dies, and life together settles down to a deadening existence.

Do you take an active interest in what means the most to your husband? Just because it is not important to you, does not mean you cannot cultivate an interest in something he cares about. Most women love to be mentally stimulated. You will find that, with the *right attitude* toward what is vital to your husband, his interests will become more and more stimulating and worthwhile to you.

Many women who were keen mentally while in school or during courtship forget the importance of keeping their minds active, growing and alert. When babies are coming one after another, it is difficult to do much reading. You feel tired and can hardly find the time or the energy to read. Once you slip into this rut, it is easy to be unaware of your husband's mental needs. Some men want to forget their work and love to hear all about the children and what happened to the neighbor. Other husbands are bored by "women-talk" and wait for the children to be put to bed so they can talk without interruption. He may want to think aloud on some aspect of his work. Perhaps he'd like your fresh viewpoint on some problem he is facing. A woman doesn't have to be brilliant to talk intelligently with her husband, nor does she need an equal education, but she does need to be alert.

> Margaret hasn't nearly the knowledge her husband has, but he has come more and more to depend on her judgment. In the evening, when the children are in bed, his usually talkative wife asks him quietly how his day has gone. Many a time he has been able to share some problem and feel the load lifted by her sympathetic interest. When faced with complicated problems, Margaret breathes a silent prayer for wisdom. At times her good judgment has changed a situation. She feels keenly the responsibility for what she says.

Referring to the ideal wife, Solomon says she "opens her mouth with wisdom and the law of kindness is on her tongue." Not only has she the wisdom to know when to speak and when to listen, but she has learned *how* to say what is needed.

Perspective

There are times a husband can lose his perspective in a difficult situation. If his wife is not personally involved, she can often help him to look at the issues more objectively. Perhaps his boss put him down at work. He may be angry, discouraged, or fearful. A few words of godly wisdom can do much to soothe his hurt and allay his fears.

On the other hand, when a wife sides with her husband and adds her anger to his, she can drag her husband down and make an already bad situation worse. During such trying experiences he needs your understanding and objective insight.

Joel's demanding job often involved problems. But when he returned home, his wife poured out her many complaints for the day. Each sympathized with the other over the wrongs of the world. Both are now in poor health. Neither has thought to challenge the other to find God's answers for their relationships to people. They could be a lovely couple with a delightful sense of humor and a blessing to many in their sphere of influence. Instead, they are turning more and more in upon themselves. It is depressing to be in their home.

Mental stimulus not only includes thinking through a situation, encouraging one's life partner to be his highest and best, but it also means continually reading challenging books.

Books on organization have helped me to make better use of my time. Recently I read a book on listening and it is fun to practice the art more successfully on my husband! Many times a wife can cull the best out of books and magazines for her busy husband. Reading can stimulate worthwhile conversation at the dinner table. Mother brought us up on *Reader's Digest* articles, and *Time* magazine. We discussed together the latest historical events. Daddy did not have time for the same sort of reading, but he could contribute to the conversation. What an influence the wife has on table talk. It takes effort to keep the conversation interesting to all and include each member of the family. At mealtime many worthwhile life principles can be instilled into children by directing stimulating table conversation.

Some husbands need encouragement to further their

education by correspondence or night school. Others need encouragement to read books that would make them more effective in their work. What a person does well he can always do better. There are shortcuts to be learned, more effective ways of organizing the home or the office, new insights into understanding people. There are fascinating ways to save time and enjoy a relaxing hobby. In all this, and more, a wife can stimulate her husband.

There is no area of life into which a couple should "settle down." We have only one life. Time is flying by. There are many with whom we have not yet shared our faith. It is even a challenge to learn how to entertain in a relaxed atmosphere and to share with others the things we are learning. Stimulating conversation with guests can often open a whole new world of ideas.

Even silent husbands, if encouraged, like to talk about their areas of interest. It is easy for a wife to take over and even answer for her husband while he is gathering his thoughts on the subject. A quick-thinking wife may need to learn to wait for her more deliberate, organized husband. There are some occasions when you can see that the conversation is flowing all around your husband and he is not taking part. When you know he has something interesting to say, you could turn to one of the group and say, "Joe was telling me the most interesting thing the other day. . . ." Then Joe can shine and you know others will appreciate what he has to say. A shoe salesman would know interesting things about leather and synthetics, a grocer understands trends in marketing, a floor covering man appreciates the latest in carpeting, and a minister is concerned about solutions for meeting the needs of our day.

Only a wife in tune with the times, her home, her church, and her husband's needs can be a continual challenge. Her vital awareness and stimulus will encourage him to be his best in every area of living.

Chapter Three

Mental Stimulus in Marriage

Questions to Ask Yourself

— Do you stimulate your husband to be his best mentally?

— What can you read to help him more? (Not necessarily his technical books but books about other fields of interest.)

— What would he like to see changed in you that would make you more of a stimulus to him? Write it down in your notebook and ask God to show you how to start changing *today*.

— How will you express today, in words, your loving pride in your husband's work and in his ability to progress in both knowledge and performance?

Peter, speaking for Jesus Christ, charges us to "gird up the loins of your minds . . ." (1 Peter 1:13).

SIDE THREE: SEXUAL FULFILLMENT

A frantic voice came over the phone from some distance, "Oh, Jill, this is Dora, pray for my husband. I just found out that he is seeing another woman and . . . it's my neighbor. Pray for me. What'll I do? Pray that he'll see how wrong he is and what this will do to our children. . . . He even wants to leave me!"

Her words were nearly incoherent as they gushed out with tears of shock, puzzled bitterness and anguish. I felt helpless, but promised to pray.

Weeks later Dora called again. "I just had to call you again. The Lord has answered our prayers, but Jill, not the way I was praying. I want you to tell other women so they won't make the same mistake I did. It was all *my* fault, Jill, it really was. God showed me how wrong I had been. I've been as blind as a bat. I've been holding out on my husband. Sex wasn't all that important to me, so I've been blind to Stanley's need. . . . I've been so involved with church and running to meetings, I didn't see or want to see that Stanley needed me. Anyway, I was usually too tired . . . the kids, the house . . . you know how it is. What a way to learn a lesson! But Jill, tell the women that a man has a far greater need for sex than a woman and if she isn't careful he will find someone else and it will be all *her* fault."

Understanding Sexual Differences

Dora put her finger on the sore spot in many marriages — the lack of understanding, appreciating and meeting a husband's sexual need. Few women really understand the difference in the makeup of men and women. Women often can channel their sex drives into some satisfying work either in the home or out of it. Their needs are more emotional and can be satisfied outside of themselves in other worthwhile pursuits. This is a God-given, protective provision which makes it possible for some women to be thoroughly happy without sexual gratification.

The makeup of a man is different. His needs are strongly physical with a God-given sexual drive for love and procreation.

One of the differences between husbands and wives is illustrated by their attitudes toward sex when they are physically tired. Sex is usually the last thing a wife wants when she's tired, but it provides her husband with the relaxation he needs for restoring sleep. Some women prefer sex at night while some men prefer to begin the day with this gratifying experience. Another difference is that after a quarrel a woman looks for *words* of reconciliation, but a man often looks for sex to heal the breach and restore the oneness with his wife. Someone stated the difference this way: "A man gives love for sex; a woman gives sex for love."

Understanding and accepting how your sex needs differ from your husband's can prevent a lot of heartache.

Understanding Your Attitudes

Men laugh about not understanding women, but truthfully, how many women understand themselves? Do you understand *yourself*? Your attitudes? Do you know why you feel as you do? Do you have a wholesome attitude toward sex? Do you know why you have your particular attitudes? Why does certain behavior from your husband bring unaccountable reactions from you?

Lack of understanding yourself can pose a lot of problems for your husband. A wife can blame her husband for problems stemming from her own subconscious attitude. Some women were taught for years that sex was wrong and that they should set up safeguards against their sex drive. Then the marriage ceremony is supposed to change everything overnight. Many women find it hard to flip over their thinking this quickly. Having been on guard for years, it is now difficult to be free.

The Power of Sexual Surrender, by Marie N. Robinson, M.D., is an excellent book for women. She helps them to see how many of their hang-ups started. Dr. Robinson, a psychiatrist, helps women overcome frigidity and see their thrilling role as wife and homemaker. She gives valuable insights into a husband's point of view.

Even though God has created men with a greater physical need for sex than women, the sex act alone does not provide him with the emotional gratification so vital to a satisfying marriage relationship.

The sex role of a woman includes much more than just physical submission — "doing her duty" by merely acquiescing to her husband's sexual demands. This

55

alone can be deadening to a husband. At times it is hard for a wife to give herself freely and endearingly to her husband, but unless she does, only physical gratification will result. When a wife understands her husband's deeper need, she can ask God for the ability to give herself wholeheartedly. A life of complete togetherness is deep and rich. Hearts are united when each partner gives himself unreservedly to the other in the act of love. Even more gratifying to a husband is having his wife initiate the sex act. To him this communicates her delight in his manhood, making him feel desirable and, above all, shows her deep appreciation of him as a lover.

Preoccupied Husbands

Most women, deeply and happily in love with their husbands, thoroughly enjoy the reciprocal thrill of married love. But there are times when different attitudes can seriously impair this feeling of oneness for a wife. For example, your husband is busy about his own affairs all day and busy about the affairs of the home all evening. Then, exhausted, he flops down to read his book or watch TV. You've been busy too, washing, shopping, refereeing kids. You had listened hopefully for your partner — the one for whom you held the fort all day. Then he's home . . . but preoccupied. So . . . dinner, dishes, babies to bed, and at last you too flop down exhausted. Does he commend you, sympathize, smile and say warm words of love and appreciation? No, he's lost in his book, still as far away as if he were at the office. And when he does look up with a yawn, it's "Honey, what have you got to eat before we go to bed?" You smile, go to the kitchen, fix his snack and then tidy up while he trudges off to bed. When you get there he's comfortably settled — reading! You crawl in, disgusted, and shut your eyes. Off goes the light and suddenly he's ready for sex. Who needs it!

It's just one more unwelcomed demand. You're too tired. He's failed you miserably. All he wants you for is to *use* you. So, as a "good" wife, you grit your teeth and submit.

But your husband's sexual appetite can't be met mechanically and dutifully, as his physical appetite can. He feels a deep emotional hunger if he isn't being satisfied through *total* unity with his wife.

There are times and circumstances when most of us feel unappreciated and "used," but we forget that men often feel the same way. Your husband may feel used, abused — a paycheck. But remember, these negative times come to nearly everyone. They should not be allowed to sour the atmosphere of your marriage.

Communicating Through Sex

A woman needs to realize that, when communication during the day is scarce with her husband, sex is an avenue of communication that is deep and meaningful to him. A man may not *say* much, but his attitude will speak volumes if you have the eyes to see and the ears to hear.

The trouble is we get defensive and resentful and focus on what he isn't rather than on what he *is* — on what he doesn't do rather than on what he *does do*. There is good advice in the Bible. It tells us to focus on what is honorable, lovable and praiseworthy (Philippians 4:8). Remember, how you feel, or how you feel *he* feels is not necessarily the way it is! Your husband comes home from a day of tension and compromises to a home of responsibility. He loves you and expects you to *know* he needs a few minutes to shut out the world and collect himself. He expects you to be just as eager to use the few precious, private minutes before sleep to lavish your love on one another. In his mind this is a settled thing, not requiring explanation or preparation.

He doesn't know your world is completely the reverse.
How can he unless you tell him?

He doesn't come crying to you about the stresses and strains of his work, how frustrated he gets or how tired. Nor does he complain because he is needed at home, or that his paycheck goes to everyone but to him. It's all part of living and marriage. It never enters his head that your needs are different or that you may be frustrated.

> One husband learned with sudden shock of his wife's daily needs when she became ill. They had a new baby and a toddler, and he found himself on the weekend in charge of his home. With proper male competence and assurance, he ordered his wife to relax in bed. He'd take care of her and everything. Slowly, his assured stride increased to a run and then a harried rush. Finally, on the second day, he fell wearily into a rocker beside his wife's bed, clutching the baby and his bottle. "Whew," he exclaimed, "Now I see what *you* have to *do!* I see why mothers rock their babies — you get a little chance to sit and rest!"

Building Sexual Unity

How are you to keep pace with your husband and make your sex life warm and continuously building toward unity? Suppose he has been ugly to you or the children today, and you're still smarting from this at bedtime. He's forgotten all about it, or maybe he's sorry and wants to show his love.

> You don't want sex,
> > You want an apology.
> > You don't want love,
> > > You want to get even.

A little coolness at this point can do it too!

But you can't build a happy marriage on resentful attitudes. You can't give love if you feel bitter. You *must forgive* the hurt before love will flow and nothing

58

but a miracle can change your attitude. Ask God for His miracle of a forgiving, loving heart. Not, "I've got to, so, God, help me," but "I want to forgive him and love him. Please, God, enable me." Although you may *not want* to forgive, you *do* want to build happiness and strength into your marriage. Remember, the power of God created and holds the universe together. Will not His power create a new attitude in your heart when you sincerely ask Him to?

Maybe you're *tired* and your husband's sex needs are too frequent and badly timed. Here again, turn to God, ask for His strength and adequate love. One woman I know faced this frustrating experience by prayerfully asking herself, *What do I have to do that is more important than taking this opportunity to strengthen the bonds of our marriage?* Another woman, whose husband's nightly demands frustrated her, found that when she entered fully into sharing love with her husband, the rich emotional satisfaction he received reduced his sexual needs from daily to two or three times a week!

No Desire for Sex

Perhaps you approach intercourse with distaste or revulsion — a conscious or subconscious feeling that sex is dirty and vulgar. Many things contribute to this common attitude in women. In the Bible it says, "God saw everything that he had made and . . . it was very good" (Genesis 1:31). Share your feelings with God. You could say to Him, "God, You created me and my husband and planned sex as the good and ultimate expression of love between us. I can't seem to find the good and the desirable in sex, Lord. I feel it is dirty and vulgar. Please show me the full beauty and joy in sharing sexual love with my husband." Thank God for His undertaking and choose to concentrate on the fact that God created sex pure and good.

It may be some of the things which are troubling you

59

should be talked over with your husband. Open lines of communication are important in establishing a good, understanding sexual relationship. Your attitude may not be wrong, but the hindrance to sex may be a legitimate problem such as a fear of pregnancy. Perhaps you feel your family is big enough now, or you can't afford another child. Your "suffering through" sex will not keep you from becoming pregnant! You and your husband should thoughtfully discuss what the arrival of more children involves — financially, emotionally, spiritually and practically. Discuss together the time and the money involved in training children for the difficult time in which we live.

Contraception

It is important for you and your husband to reach an agreement regarding contraception. If you are not comfortable with the methods you now use, pray for the right time and the right words to discuss openly a better way for both of you. You may want to experiment to see what meets your individual need best. Once you have gained confidence in talking over these problem areas, you will find a new freedom and openness with your husband.

A man and wife really begin to communicate when they come to share a *desire to understand* each other and the problems each faces. Understanding does not necessarily mean agreeing. Without understanding, however, agreement isn't even possible. Until you see eye to eye regarding your family planning, you need to be inwardly free to accept God's twofold purpose for marriage — a life together and bearing children.

Make time to be alone with each other so you can talk. In our rushed society this is hard, but it shows how important each of you is to the other. Then you can think of ways which will bring more pleasure into your relationship. When sex is not a last-minute, on-the-run need to be satisfied, it will enhance the enjoyment of your love for each other. It is an art for a wife to express her desire for her husband and yet not demand his love in such a way as to make him feel inadequate in meeting her need. It brings rich fulfillment to a man to know his wife wants him to share the deepest expression of his love to her.

An Important Discovery

Years ago I stumbled onto an important discovery. The life drive and the sex drive are linked. When the sex drive is frustrated it often hinders the life drive. There are men who are able to bypass a poor marriage relationship and attain their life goals, but this is difficult. A man's sexuality is an important aspect of his self-image, and failure in this area is apt to erode his self-esteem and hinder success in his life work.

Janice was desperate for help. It was from her that I learned the seriousness of frigidity. Her story unfolded with confusion. Her eyes were clouded, and with much difficulty she explained her problem. "My stepfather took advantage of me when I was a teenager," she told me with deep bitterness. "I hate him. I can't stand for my husband to approach me — my stepfather looms between us."

What could I say? I asked God for His wisdom. The Lord's Prayer came into my mind. "Forgive us our debts as we forgive our debtors," as we forgive those who trespass against us. I struggled within myself. *Ask her to forgive when she had been so wronged? It seemed utterly unreasonable, but God was speaking.*

"You have to forgive your stepfather," I told her. Then I reminded her of our Lord's Prayer which she knew so well.

"I can't," she said dejectedly.

"You must. It's the only way. If you don't forgive you cannot receive God's forgiveness. He says He will forgive us our debts *as we forgive others."*

As Janice and I talked, part of the time she looked like she understood; at other times her attention drifted. I left discouraged.

Weeks later Janice sent for me. I scarcely recognized the woman who greeted me warmly at the door.

"I just had to tell you, Jill. I've forgiven my stepfather! I will tell him the next time he and my mother visit. It didn't seem wise to write it to him.

"And Jill, I asked God to blot out that awful memory. It's hard to believe what has happened between my husband and me! We have a new love for each other. . . . And something else — Ed's boss called me and wanted to know what I'd done for Ed. He is a new man at work and has become so good at his job he's become invaluable to his boss!"

Janice's lovely eyes were clear and bright — her speech no longer jumbled. I realized how close she had been to a mental breakdown. During subsequent visits it was thrilling to watch the whole family grow spiritually, to hear of their answers to prayer and their fresh love for Christ and the Bible.

A wife may demonstrate her love in innumerable other ways but it is often negated by her rejection, or lack of enjoyment of sex. To a man, sex is the most meaningful demonstration of love and self-worth. A husband's gift of sexual pleasure is full of meaning. It's a part of his own deepest person. How his wife receives him has a much more profound effect on him than most women realize. To receive him with joy and to share sexual pleasure builds into him a sense of being worthy, desirable and acceptable. To reject him, to tolerate him and to put him off as unimportant tears at the very center of his self-esteem.

What happiness it is to experience a wholesome attitude toward sex. You do not need to have had a good atmosphere in the home in which you grew up, because God can change your attitude and heal your memories. God created sex in all purity, and it is only the misuse of it which has made it ugly. God has such a thrilling role for us as wives; it is a shame to mar it with wrong concepts and the memory of unhappy childhood experiences.

When two people become one in love, each is able to come far closer to his full potential. Each begins to blossom and develop under the influence of warm acceptance. There is no competition, no domination. God's commandment to love your neighbor as yourself becomes reality.

Understanding love dispels the crushing fear of ridicule or of being unacceptable. Your total "givingness" can free your loved one to express the secret dreams and desires that are hidden deep within. Once freed emotionally, he also finds increased effectiveness in other areas of his life.

Take heart. *It takes time and a deep desire* for a husband and wife to find complete happiness and unity. Your needs are so different. It takes God-given understanding, patience and love to merge two lives into one. If you seek with all your heart, you will find God's wonderful intention for your marriage. Remember, outlook and sex needs differ. Study each other. Some couples have found happiness after twenty or more years!

A practical book which has been of great help to many couples is *Sexual Happiness in Marriage* by Herbert J. Miles (published by Zondervan Publishing House, Grand Rapids, Michigan). This book clarifies the basic sex differences between men and women and explains how each can satisfy the other in their sex relationship.

Chapter Three
Sexual Fulfillment in Marriage

Questions to Ask Yourself

— What could be marring your husband's full sexual happiness? What can you do to change this? When?

— What are the differences between you and your husband in sexual expression? List in detail the difference in timing, outlook, attitude, frequency, etc.

— As you "listen" for his needs, how can you adapt yourself to meet them?

— Isolate one wrong attitude you have toward sex and concentrate on changing it by God's help.

— When can you plan time this week to be alone with your husband just to enjoy each other?

"Do not refuse . . . each other (. . . your . . . marital rights), except . . . by mutual consent . . . lest Satan tempt you to sin through . . . sexual desire" (1 Corinthians 7:5, *Amplified Bible*).

SIDE FOUR: EMOTIONAL SATISFACTION

The emotional side of life is not easily defined, for it is the deep, feeling side of a person. Feelings can be expressed by joy or anger, peace or frustration. The same circumstances can produce completely different feelings in a husband than in his wife. For example, one person enjoys being alone, while another person is restless and fearful when alone. The way you and your husband react to the same circumstances depends largely on your temperaments and early training. To create a happy emotional climate for your husband requires observation and study of his emotional reactions.

- What makes him sad or glad?
  - What triggers his anger?
    - What fills him with frustration?
      - What gives him feelings of deep satisfaction?

Emotions, developed rightly, foster harmony and unity in marriage. During times of relaxation, the bonds of marriage can be strengthened. Emotional needs of a husband and wife can be met by spending time together. Relaxation gives opportunity for free communication. Just to enjoy each other and to share freely brings deep pleasure as well as deeper understanding. In our complex society couples have to make a concerted effort to spend time alone. A marriage which is developing unity could fall apart without it. Time effectively spent together is vital to a happy marriage.

I read a story many years ago that opened my eyes to how easy it is for a wife to overlook the feelings of her husband and be completely blind to what is deeply meaningful to him. Polly's story alerted me to think about what was important to my husband's happiness but not really important to me.

Polly, an attractive, intelligent, well-dressed wife, began to settle comfortably into a middle-aged rut. For almost two years there had been little to disturb her life with Herb. They were enjoying their New England home and the fun of decorating a new house after twenty years in New York. Herb had climbed up the "ladder of success" so they were enjoying financial security.

One cool Friday evening Herb came home from the office, greeting her enthusiastically with, "Honey, I have to fly to New York in two weeks for some company board meetings. I would really love to have you along. We could go to Carnegie Hall. At last we have a chance to do some of the 'fun things' we've had to pass up all these years. After the committee meetings we'll have the evenings together. You know how much I've wanted to hear J. H. on the violin. It would mean so much to have you along."

Polly's heart sank. There was still so much to do since they had moved. There were things she could finish while he was away. What a bother to have to pack and unpack again. "Oh, honey, wouldn't you concentrate better and finish sooner if I stayed home?"

Herb's eyes clouded. "If that's what you want," he answered in a flat tone as he walked away. The anticipation of a work-holiday with his wife collapsed.

The next day Polly heard a car coming up their long drive. She wondered who it could be. Walking quickly to the beautiful bay window, Polly watched curiously as a red convertible parked by the front steps. An attractive young woman stepped out.

Polly gasped — *Carol! Herb's former secretary! She had been in love with Herb. . . . What could she want?*

Polly graciously welcomed Carol, and Herb greeted her enthusiastically. Polly then took her through their new home. As they went from room to room Polly wondered. *Why is she here? It's been almost two years since she's seen Herb. . . . What does she want?* Her mind was in a turmoil.

At lunchtime Polly invited Carol to join them and she accepted eagerly. During lunch there was still no indication as to why Carol had come. The mealtime passed quickly, filled with small talk and the latest news. But Polly was uneasy.

After clearing the table and doing dishes, Polly suggested that Herb entertain Carol while she went grocery shopping. As she hurried out the door she turned to Carol, "Since you've come so far, why don't you spend the night?" Again Polly's invitation was accepted.

As she picked up loaves of bread and weighed the oranges that were on sale, Polly's mind wrestled with agonizing questions. *Why has she come? Is she still in love with Herb? I wonder what they are talking about.*

That evening Polly tried to make dinner a festive occasion and the evening an enjoyable one. They retired late. In bed Polly lay wondering.

Herb was noncommittal about Carol's visit. He dropped off to sleep as Polly stared into the darkness, unable to relax.

After breakfast the next morning, a radiant Carol was ready to leave. Polly, still mystified about Carol's purpose in coming, walked to the red convertible with her. Suddenly Carol threw her arms around Polly, exclaiming, "Thanks so much for letting me stay and especially for yesterday afternoon. You know how much I've thought of Herb. Being alone with him helped me to settle my feelings about him. Our new manager asked me to marry him. I just had to be sure."

Polly breathed a sigh of relief. *How foolish I've been to be so absorbed in my comfort at home while Herb attends dry board meetings and spends his evenings alone. How easy it would be to lose him while I selfishly stay home.*

Polly came alive with her new insight. The importance of being with Herb, when he wanted her, became a new joy in her life. Why it could be a second honeymoon! Polly, all aglow, turned to Herb, "Honey, when is it *we* leave for New York?"

Not responding happily to unexpected or unplanned times together could prove devastating to a marriage. Refusing to share these opportunities to be with your husband can communicate rejection. He may feel that you do not really enjoy his companionship.

Differing Preferences

The recreation and relaxation which provides emotional satisfaction for a husband and wife may differ widely. One may prefer to stay home, while the other wants to socialize. One may like to read, while the other prefers golf or a drive in the country. Finding some mutual pleasure is not always easy, but very important. This involves give and take and at times the "give" takes a lot of adjustment for a wife whose tastes differ from her husband's.

Differing tastes give a creative wife an opportunity to accept these differences and to find mutually agreeable outlets. There are wives who have taken up golf or learned to fish to eliminate a conflict of interests. However, if you don't care for your husband's hobby, try to interest him in yours. There is no harm in trying — *in the right spirit.* Sometimes women want to have their husbands enjoy *their* friends, *their* idea of fun, without considering their husband's tastes. Often when a wife has gone all out to involve herself in her husband's recreation, he has in turn become interested in what she enjoys.

There are times when a husband and wife can "agree to disagree" regarding recreation. It could do your husband a world of good to spend a day at the golf course with his friends. Anticipating and preparing for his return with candlelight and silver could be a delightful experience. For some other men an occasional night out with "the boys" provides an enjoyable, refreshing time.

One woman I know loves to travel. Her husband prefers gardening. He lets his wife go freely because he sees what it does for her. She in turn is thrilled to get home to him and their beautiful flowers.

Relaxing together cements a relationship and pays tremendous dividends. With life today so hectic, a wife must carefully guard these times of togetherness.

The stress in the work-world today makes it imperative for a wife to be alert to her husband's need for rest and change. It often takes much prayer and planning ahead to free a busy husband from his work, even for a weekend. It also takes creative management to arrange your budget to provide your husband with maximum renewal — and, if possible, with the opportunity to re-evaluate his schedule to find the most satisfying way to use his time.

A young wife was deeply concerned with her husband's long hours. After much prayer she shared her concern with a friend. The friend offered to keep their two children for a weekend. Her husband chose a trip to a scenic spot a comfortable drive away. That trip became beneficial in more ways than just rest and change.

They visited friends who added a surprise element to the trip, urging them to accept a job in the town! They returned happily several months later to live there.

Heart Communication

Even the most sociable of husbands and wives need time alone with each other, time to talk from the heart and time to listen *without preoccupation.* You can work toward a deeper understanding of the hopes and fears each of you has. Make an effort to draw out of your husband how he feels about himself, his life and goals for the family. He will see that his interests are important to you, thus deepening the bond between you.

Are you fulfilling your earlier dreams, or have you been subconsciously caught in the mad materialistic rush for security? Does he really know in his heart that you accept the work which makes him happy and that this is far more important to you than a job which could make him wealthy? Does he know that you have confidence in his ability and do not consider less pay to mean less ability or less intelligence?

Are you, as parents, meeting your children's changing needs? What can you do to be more adequate parents?

Have you been living superficially? Drifting? What activities should you discuss dropping to relieve a pressured home life so you can make a more vital contribution to your children?

Look over your life as it is. Are you satisfied with what you see? Have you unwittingly been competing with one another? Do you really have to prove something? How can you turn your spirit of competition

69

into support? How can you fit your gifts together, rather than using them separately?

I'd like to add quickly that there is no harm in pursuing different interests. Your very differences can strengthen your marriage and help to make you a couple with a broader scope of influence. A wife's sincere appreciation of her husband's skills, and her encouragement of them can keep away the spirit of competition and create an added challenge for him to excel in his field.

> One woman I know was afraid to venture into a work which could have been competitive with her husband's. Her husband freely encouraged her to use her gifts. In her full life of work and home, she was always careful to keep the various facets of her life balance. As time went on, she discovered that many of the things she learned on her job gave her a deeper understanding of her husband's work and a deeper appreciation of his abilities. There were many opportunities when the wife's new concepts enabled her to identify with her husband's world more fully and satisfyingly.

Male Emotional Cycles

Did you know that men have emotional cycles too?* The cycle usually changes every two weeks, but their "moods" seem more pronounced once a month. I have read that many businessmen are aware of these cycles and will not make important decisions during their low points. With some men these moods are more obvious. During these times they need special, tolerant understanding. You may find that your husband sinks periodically into gloom and discouragement for seemingly no reason at all. His responsibilities at work trouble him and he tends to lose his perspective. From his

---

Time Magazine, August 31, 1970, page 7, "Rarely publicized male condition . . . cycle every 51-55 days . . . Nice men became monsters . . . some decisions made . . . hastily changed." Hargreaves, Industrial Health Consultant.

warped, emotional perspective, even ordinary home situations create a crisis.

It would help both of you to clock his cycles. Then, when he is in a better frame of mind, you can show him that his depressions come and go on schedule. Their regularity can be clocked on the calendar. He can see for himself that his moods are caused by his emotional low cycle — not by you or problems at work. He will see that between moods he can more than adequately handle you or problems at work.

You will know when to sympathetically laugh away his fears and when to listen understandingly. Our loving God can give His divine wisdom for the times your husband needs extra support and patience. Your creative love and understanding will be a special source of strength for his emotional well-being during these times.

Your Personal Identity

Deep emotional satisfaction comes to both men and women when they clearly maintain their own identities. How proud a husband is of his thoroughly feminine wife. Somehow it draws out all his manliness. As one commercial puts it: *Want him to be more of a man? Then be more of a woman!* A helpless woman may seem more feminine, but there is nothing unfeminine about being capable. Femininity depends on a woman's attitude to herself and to men. The pressure of "women's rights" make some women feel overwhelmed by a loss of identity and the uselessness of a woman's role. Extremes in seeking to do away with the differences between the sexes will never lessen the importance of a woman being thoroughly a woman — and loving every minute of it!

Sometimes we learn more from seeing the negative than the positive. Have you seen the attitude of the wife in an unhappy home? What do you see in the wife's attitude that turns off her husband or fills him with

71

resentment? Now, looking at yourself objectively, what do you see your attitude doing to your husband.

Do you resent your role as a woman? Do you envy a man's role? Why? Are your reasons valid? Some women confuse femininity with stupidity and consider the role of homemaking as something any nitwit could do. But the mess so many homes are in is proof enough that happy homemaking is no easy job.

Watch women who are adored by their husbands. What is the secret of their success? Notice their attitude toward their own roles and toward their husbands as men and fathers. What *principles* do you see that would make you a better wife?

What a challenge to work toward a deep emotional satisfaction in marriage which comes from complete sharing in every area of life. This would include

- a vital faith
  - mental stimulus
    - a mutually satisfying sexual relationship
      - and fun-filled free times just to enjoy each other!

Chapter Three

Emotional Satisfaction in Marriage

Questions to Ask Yourself

— What are your husband's emotional needs?
— What upsets his emotional well-being? When?
— What would make his life and your marriage happier?
— What simple recreation could you plan to have together *this week* to enrich your relationship?

"Love is patient and kind . . . does not keep a record of wrongs. . . . Love never gives up: its faith, hope and patience never fail" (1 Corinthians 13:4-7, *Good News for Modern Man*).

Part Two:

Understanding Yourself

4
The Real You

Self-acceptance

"I hate myself. I always have. I hate my size and my looks. I hate the way I am," sobbed Ann bitterly over the phone.

Ann's attitude toward herself was causing trouble at work. She frequently felt people were picking on her. Actually, she received more love and consideration than many women.

My heart went out to Ann. If only I could convey to her the excitement of life with her "self" given over to God. How could I show her the miraculous change that can come into a woman's life when her Creator has His full way . . .

- when bitterness toward God (for making her thus) is confessed and forgiven . . .
  - when the peace and later the joy of self-acceptance come.

There is no limit to what God can do to transform a woman inwardly and make her life one of fulfillment outwardly, when He can have His way!

The full import of the thrill of being a woman in the hands of a perfectly loving God has taken me years to realize. Only recently I heard a significant statement which put into words what I feel God will do:

"The Holy Spirit releases the full creativity of each woman, so she can find her own medium for the expression of God through her individual life." No one needs to be a carbon copy of anyone else! Each woman is

God's own original creation to fit the particular sphere in life that He has designed for her. Just think . . .

What will God create through *you*?

The Bible has its own vivid way of explaining this truth. It describes a potter making a vessel. He sees the lump of clay in his hand (Jeremiah 18:3-6), but in his mind is a beautifully finished vase, unlike any other that he has made. Sometimes the clay is marred so the potter then reshapes the vessel to fit another purpose. The new vessel is then redesigned for its greatest usefulness.

It is amazing what God can do with a "lump" of clay when it is turned over to Him! He will form each one into the finest instrument to function in the circumstances He has in mind. Too often we groan helplessly about ourselves as "ugly lumps," when we should let God transform us into what He knows we can become.

Self-acceptance has been a long process for me. It came in different areas of my life over a long period of time. I can't remember anyone really talking to me about the vital importance of accepting myself.

My own awareness of God's love for me *personally* and the need to accept myself came to me in college. After I realized this personal love and saw, in part, the needlessness of a deep inferiority complex, I began to live! However, it has taken years to bring specific areas of my life into God's transforming truth, to see the miracle of what He could do with my life as I yielded to His molding.

Looking Back

My self-acceptance seemed to be an outgrowth of turning my life over to God the summer after my junior year in high school. This was not easy for me. I had my own dreams and ambitions and I had an erroneous concept of Christianity. The seeming boredom and

76

restrictions of a dedicated Christian life filled me with dread. I dreamed of a future of exciting, self-gratifying pleasure, fascinating travel abroad, and of dating men of the world. All this seemed far more exciting than the dull routine of prayer, Bible study and going out with preachers' sons. The curtain of time hid the thrill of the God-planned life that awaited me . . .

- a godly husband
  - wonderful children
    - rewarding work
      - meaningful world travel

During my senior year of high school in Korea, I began to experience the joy of praying with my friends and seeing God answer us. As president of the young people's group it was exciting to plan relevant and meaningful meetings. Interest in these gatherings increased all year. Other young people awakened to spiritual realities and were challenged to commit their lives to Christ. Young people were filled with purpose as they saw the need to prepare daily for a useful life ahead. It was a worthwhile and deeply satisfying year.

Returning to the United States for college, I felt very insecure and out of place. But after four years, I saw another aspect of self-acceptance. I had to accept the fact that I was different from girls born and reared in America. I needed to let go the feeling of frustration and accept my own uniqueness in outlook. This gave birth to a new freedom with people.

Another step of self-acceptance came years later when I married a man who was born with a beautiful spirit. I began to resent even more my own irritable disposition. I had spiritual battles which were foreign to my husband. Then God taught me a further lesson: *to accept my temperament* and to look to God to make me what He wanted me to be. Since then, and as I continue to mature in the Christian life, I see God enabling me to encourage people *because* of my own struggles. It is exciting to see that the very differences between my husband and me now strengthen our ministry and enable us to reach more people with the glorious message that Jesus Christ accepts each of us as we are and uses those very differences.

How?

Self-acceptance is so simple, yet so profound that we stumble over it. Thank God for yourself,

> your size,
>> your way,
>>> your disposition,
>>> your education,
>>> your abilities,
>>>> your background.

Present yourself, as you are, to the living, loving God, your Father. Expect Him to begin the molding process. It will come through circumstances. Accept them in faith. God will use each one. The Holy Spirit will supply the power to live, within your circumstances, a godly, worthwhile, fulfilling life. A change in attitude toward yourself can come *overnight,* but the outworking in your daily circumstances is a growing, maturing, and *life-long process*.

When a woman cannot accept herself, it is hard for her to believe that others accept her. This attitude can be a terrible drain on her husband and friends. There are husbands who have to spend a great deal of time building up their insecure wives, when both of them could be getting on with the work God has given them to do.

Hildah was one of three children. Her brother, four years younger, was brilliant. Her father constantly compared her to this brother, often calling her stupid. He tried to mold her after his ideas, which Hildah could never quite fulfill. In trying to cook his favorite foods, she lacked her mother's skill. Then, to top it all off, at fourteen she grew to be five feet nine inches tall, taller than all of her schoolmates — a freak! As a result of this combination of factors, Hildah became a shy introvert.

When Hildah was ten, she asked Jesus Christ to come into her heart, but the real turning point came at seventeen, when at camp she turned her life over to the Lord. In time she began to see the foolishness of being a wallflower, of resenting her height, and of feeling inferior about her intelligence. She accepted the fact that God had not shortchanged her.

With this change in attitude, Hildah began to be outgoing in her youth group. She was elected president, even dated a short boy and wore "flats." She began to use her mind. At first she carried her new attitude to an extreme. It took time for her to find the balance between being a wallflower and making a spectacle of herself as the life of the party.

Today Hildah has developed another gift — singing. In the early days love for singing was not recognized as a gift. Now her lovely voice fills the room — and the hearts of people — as she sings for her Lord, free from damaging self-consciousness.

She is now the creative wife of Jim, a busy executive (incidentally, he's tall) and the mother of four sons. She finds this a satisfying career. After a long day at work, Jim returns to his wife who is often outfitted in her own latest creation. She greets him warmly at the door. The aroma of a delicious meal comes tantalizingly from the kitchen.

"Oh, darling, you're wonderful!" he exclaims enthusiastically as he embraces her.

Accepting Your Temperament

A woman needs to accept herself *in order to be accepted.* God tells us in Romans 12:3 that we are not to "think of ourselves more highly than we ought to think," but to "think soberly," that is, consider ourselves realistically. A quiet woman is to accept her quiet temperament without resenting the fact she can't be like her lively friends. The enthusiastic wife needs to accept the fact that not everyone shares her zest for living.

Each temperament has its strong and weak points, but you must accept the way God made you and realize that you are best suited for your husband just the way you are. That is why he *married you.* Trying to be what God never intended you to be keeps you from the special creativity within you. Self-acceptance is an ongoing process which forms the basis for continuing maturity. It is not that you cannot or should not improve in your weak areas with God's help, but resentment over them and non-acceptance of yourself dulls your perception and keeps you from realizing your best.

Different Gifts

Martha loved to entertain, but found teaching most difficult. When she accepted her gift of hospitality, she entertained frequently. She often invited those who had shared their problems with her along with guests who had found some helpful answers.

Mary, on the other hand, found it hard to have guests. She felt guilty for not wanting to entertain. When she accepted her gift of teaching and used her time to study, she too became a blessing to many, *in her way.*

80

Finding Personal Fulfillment Takes Time

Begin where you are. By accepting yourself, you develop into your full potential as you find and begin to fit into God's way for you. Understanding how you function and accepting the way you function takes time. But when you begin to compare yourself with other women and try to live as they do, you smother the real, creative you.

Each area of your life offers an opportunity for learning a new facet of yourself. This becomes a lifelong process. As you adapt to your husband, and become more and more adequate as a mother, you will discover your sphere of contribution to society. You will be continuously challenged with new and different areas in which to grow.

A Realistic Attitude

Do you feel more frustrated than fulfilled? Are your personal standards realistic? For example, Sue seems to be a terrific wife. She rises early and all her work is done by ten A.M. At a morning coffee klatsch she chats happily, brightly telling you all she has done before ten.

And you? Your eyes are hardly open by ten in the morning. You feel condemned! But Sue didn't tell you how she's dragging by eight P.M. and may even be cross with her family. But you? By eight in the evening you've just started swinging! You're a happy wife and a cheerful mother — after ten A.M.! After the little ones are in bed, you can even slick up the house! Don't fight your differences. Accept them and work *with* them. Get up in time for enough coffee to get the family happily off to school and work! You don't have to clean half the house before breakfast. Make their lunches the night before. There's no virtue in sandwiches being made in the morning.

Keeping up with Sue, trying to force yourself to be

what another person is naturally, could produce frustration in your life. Unwittingly there may be other ways you are trying to mold your life according to what *people* think and punishing yourself because you can't keep up to another's standard.

Why try to furnish your home in antiques when you prefer a modern decor? Or why chafe at your present "early attic" furniture until you are able to afford what you really like? You will begin to feel more and more satisfied as you accept the home best suited to you in your circumstances. This takes thought. What way of life is most comfortable for you and your husband?

- Simplicity? No knickknacks and minimum dust?

  - A compact, modern home — because of limited strength?

    - Or an old home with enough elbow room to eliminate the nervous tension of crowding?

What is your life-style, your need?

Personal fulfillment is progressive. Accepting each stage of family living is fun. Joy comes from working continually toward a better marriage, seeing a contented husband and happy children. It is rewarding to accept each new precious baby to love, cherish and train for God. Satisfaction grows in seeing wholesome children developing into self-confident, secure adults, eager to take their place in life.

New Phase

When your children have left home, it is exciting to see how God has been preparing you to find your fulfillment now in seeing the needs of others and helping them, thus creating a new place for yourself.

82

For example, could you open your home to young people who need your love and wise counsel? Could you take time to visit lonely women in your community? What a wonderful opportunity to have prayer and Bible study with them. Also, many churches are crying for the help of women to work in their outreach programs.

Just a word of warning. The hardest thing in the world is to keep balanced. There are times when a wife finds such a wide sphere of ministry for herself that she unwittingly neglects her husband and home. The need she has created for herself creates more and more of a demand for her services. At such times the wife must learn the art of saying "No!" Her husband and home are still her first concern and she must do only what will fit happily into his schedule. Unless she maintains vigilance regarding her husband's needs, frustration will creep in again — frustration due to feeling her place in the home is not being filled adequately.

A fulfilled woman, able to keep a balance between work at home and outside, brings a sense of contentment to her marriage.

Chapter Four

The Real You

Questions to Ask Yourself

— How does self-acceptance affect your attitude toward life? Toward people? And especially toward your husband?

— What is the hardest area of your life to accept?

— What do you find the most difficult to accept about yourself?

— In seeking to see yourself as God created you:

  — What is your potential? Your likes and dislikes? Are you basically quiet or lively, a homebody or career girl?

  — How can you structure (or unstructure!) your life to suit your temperament and get from life *all* God has for you and your husband?

— How can you help your husband to understand *you* better?

— What will you share with your husband tonight to help him accept you as you are learning to accept yourself?

5
Personal Growth

Emotional Maturity

Personal growth is a lifetime enterprise! It is exciting to look back over the years to see your progress. You can see that trials — at the time so hard to accept — have been used of God to develop your character, to stabilize and strengthen your emotional life.

Emotional maturity is a hard quality to define, a quality that affects the whole atmosphere of the home. Maybe it's that quality within a woman which enables her to handle the situations in her life in a way that is helpful to herself and to all those around her. The emotionally mature woman is able to keep her equilibrium under stress and to view her situations objectively and to live with inner freedom.

Little emphasis is placed today on the old-fashioned virtue of self-control. Often it is so much easier to do impetuously what you feel like doing rather than waiting to do what you should. An emotionally mature woman is led by her will rather than by her emotions.

It is hard to think straight when your emotions are involved. It is difficult to be sweet and patient when you wake up with a headache. It seems impossible not to snap at the children when you are depressed over a misunderstanding with your husband. It is not easy to love a woman who has criticized you behind your back. These are normal reactions from which no one is immune.

We are told much today on how to become Christians, but there are few who tell us how to live an effective Christian life.

The Bible is a handbook on Christian conduct, full of illustrations of those who succeeded and those who failed and *why!* It's thrilling to know that God has not brought us into the world to flounder around in our weakness but to triumph through His strength, to do what we should do, *when* we should do it.

Drawing Daily Strength

Once you have committed your life to your Savior as Lord, you will find it a joy to spend time each day reading His Book of instructions. If you do this at a time when you can be alone for at least fifteen minutes you will begin to find the inner strength that comes from knowing God and seeking to please Him. As you pray about the things you face each day, remember that He has promised to give all the wisdom you need (James 1:5).

To the casual reader the Bible seems like a difficult Book. Therefore, each time before you read it, ask God to show you *His way* and what He means by what He has written. It is easier to start in the New Testament and perhaps even easier if you start with one of Paul's letters written to Christians. Look for God's commands. You will find that a command is nearly always followed by a wonderful promise of help or of some reward. All of God's commandments are summarized in just two:

1. Thou shalt love the Lord thy God with *all* thy heart, with *all* thy soul and with *all* thy mind. . . .

2. Thou shalt love thy neighbor as thyself (Matthew 22:37, 39).

Love-in-depth is described in First Corinthians thirteen. God's whole purpose for us is to learn to love as He loves and to live with one another as He demonstrated to us through the life of Christ when He lived on earth.

True emotional maturity is based on the solid rock of spiritual maturity. This begins with a personal relationship with Jesus Christ and a life committed to Him. It continues with a God-given self-acceptance. It grows daily as we meet each situation with His help and strength and reach out to others with His love.

God has a standard for His Kingdom here on earth. It begins in the home. When these standards are practiced in the home, parents can guide their children into Christian maturity.

A nation is nurtured in the home. It is still true that "The hand that rocks the cradle rules the world." The adequacy of that rule depends largely on the steadiness of the hand. Taking time with God and looking to Him for clear direction will bring changes in a marriage that will transform a home. Even in difficult marriages where there is little cooperation from the husband, women have been able to rear godly children with the help of God-given strength and confidence. Through the influence of these Christian homes, God can change our nation's shaky morals and weakened homes.

Controlling Tension

In our home it's not major crises that cause family tensions, it's the minor crisis where I become tense and start being pushy, setting everyone's teeth on edge. It took our German Shepherd to show me how my tension affected the whole family one hectic Sunday morning. I had not allowed enough time for all that needed to be done and had been too preoccupied the night before to see that shoes were polished and Bibles and Sunday school books were collected. After much pressure and frantic hurry, we left for church in a whirl, leaving Wong to guard the house. During church my equilibrium was restored. But when we returned home Wong did not greet us with his usual exuberance. His ears and tail drooped with guilt. We found wastebaskets upset and the contents littering the rooms. In his frustration Wong had even chewed up some of the children's stuffed animals. I scolded Wong, but in my heart I felt sure his conduct was the result of the tension he felt when we left for church.

The following week we all mended our ways. We left the house with composure and in adequate time to arrive at church. Upon our return Wong greeted us with his ears up and his tail wagging wildly. The house was as we had left it. It's pretty bad when it takes a dog to remind a wife to be calm, cool, and collected!

Husbands

Perhaps no other life-situation stretches a woman's emotional capacity more than the intimate day-to-day husband-wife relationship. It's here the second commandment is sorely tested: "Love thy neighbor as thyself." And what closer neighbor do you have than your husband? It takes maturity to submit without being a doormat, to let him have the final word when you disagree and to keep your husband first when you're tempted to put your children ahead of him. It takes maturity to think through why certain words and actions from your husband invoke such violent reactions in you. It also takes maturity to avoid saying and doing things that cause your husband to react violently. What steps would God have you take to develop emotional maturity? For what do you want God's specific help?

Handling Reverses

Are you a woman who is able to take both difficulty and success in stride? Your husband is fortunate if you can keep a right sense of values in the face of material success. He is fortunate, too, if you are able to accept reverses calmly. Do you find you are able to draw strength from God when these times come? A spiritually mature women knows God is in control of each situation and that He is fully aware of what is happening. She has full confidence that God can work through a seemingly impossible situation.

I have a friend who has gone through a tragic personal experience. Some of her friends cannot understand her quiet peace in the midst of a stormy life, but, as she confided to me, "God has taken away my hurt and given me His peace. What a wonderful opportunity I have to show others that God does give peace and you can 'rejoice always' in God's goodness."

The husbands of two of my friends lost their jobs for a few months. It was thrilling to hear how (in the case of each wife) God kept their hearts at peace as day after day there were no jobs, no money for food, but bills to be paid. For one wife, unexpected gifts were brought to the house. The other wife said to me afterwards, "I don't know how God did it, but we were even able to pay all our bills while Bob was out of work."

Another friends often told me her children belonged to the Lord and were dedicated to Him; however, it was another story when one of the girls, Joy, became critically ill. The mother was frantic with worry. Joy passed the crisis of her illness, but the doctor said the disease was incurable. That was the final blow to drive the mother closer to God. As she cast herself on God's mercy, from her heart, she gave Joy unreservedly to God for His will. In a short time God performed a miracle. Joy completely recovered (unheard of for this disease) and now, many years later, is a registered nurse, serving the Lord with her husband.

God is working out purposes far beyond what we can see. Reverses and trials can be stepping-stones to strengthen our faith and dependence upon God. Read the book of Philippians, and you can see how Paul was able to rejoice in impossible circumstances. God does not want just our natural optimism. It comes to an end when pressed too far. He wants us to trust in Him with *supernatural* faith in the midst of trial.

Because we are human it seems that unless we *have to* depend on God we can't know and trust His real dependability. God often takes away all other support *so we'll learn to count on His trustworthiness in the midst of trying times.*

> At one time our two children and I had to live in an impossible situation. The woman with whom I lived was a neurotic semi-invalid. I had to be in by nine at night. Running water after this hour was forbidden. Two hours during the mid-morning there had to be quiet with no children-noises or phone calls so she could rest. The same was true for the afternoon. After a few weeks I felt trapped. Then I read *The Robe.* A thought presented in this book illuminated my soul. A man asked the master of a slave why he could not control his slave's thinking. The master replied, "He is my slave and has to do my bidding, but *I cannot control his thinking. In his mind he is a free man.*" Suddenly I realized that freedom is in the mind, not in physical circumstances. No wonder Paul could rejoice in jail. He was a free man. The jailers could not touch his spirit.

How many times this thought has set me free in other difficult circumstances where I felt trapped! Isn't it wonderful how having the right attitude can enable you to handle a difficult situation?

Criticism

It requires maturity to take criticism. Nobody hates criticism more than I do. But I've come to realize that I cannot grow to maturity if I am not willing to see the things in me that need to be changed. So now, with

God's help (and believe me, I need His help), I *ask* my husband and children each year what they want to see changed in me. That's really a miracle! Now I've gone a step further. Since my husband cannot think of too much when I ask him on the spot, during the year I write down the things that annoy him — things like not keeping the front hall tidy, not eating meals in the dining room when we are not rushed, not keeping the front porch swept, not paying the children's allowances regularly, and not arriving at church ahead of time.

Accepting criticism with grace and profit does not come overnight, so don't be discouraged. Don't be afraid to apologize for having flared up in anger when you felt that you were being picked on. Occasionally it takes time to cool off and see the criticism in its proper perspective. It takes time to see your husband's viewpoint when it's so different from your own. There may be times when you feel threatened. You feel that your role as a wife is at stake. Send up a quick prayer to God and ask Him to keep you from saying something for which you later may be sorry. Ask Him to show you what you need to see. In time your understanding of each other will increase and your love will deepen. Criticism becomes less frequent and the little sources of frequent irritation can be anticipated and cared for quickly. Lovingly avoiding unnecessary conflict is the oil that keeps the wheels of marriage running smoothly.

Steady Disposition

The emotionally mature woman develops steady disposition. She is able to be cheerful before her cup of morning coffee as well as after 10 o'clock!

What is the key to an unhappy disposition? You may feel you were born with one, but what is your attitude toward it? Do you think it is *important* to have an even disposition?

91

I hate to admit it, but it was a long time before I was convicted of my "morning depression" which cast gloom over the whole family. One day I saw the sin of such behavior and confessed it to God. I made my feelings in the morning a matter of prayer each night. It was also my first prayer upon awakening — expecting God to change me. He did! A sluggish thyroid and all. An extra bonus came later. One of our girls commented on my change which led her to seek God to undertake for one of her problems.

We all know we shouldn't be cross with our children. "It isn't nice, it isn't Christian," you say. But at times you couldn't care less. You are at the end of your rope, exhausted. Your family suffers because you feel you can count on them to forgive and understand when you lose your temper.

Your disposition sets the climate in which your husband and children must live and grow. What effect is your selfishness having on them? Your children are the most important and most vulnerable people within your sphere of influence. They are learning from your pattern of life. What are you teaching them as they observe and learn from your reactions?

What about your husband? You think because he is an adult he should be considerate of your emotional needs. And because he is considerate, you feel free to indulge in your moods and your irritability. But what about *his* needs? You are adding the extra effort of encouraging you to his other burdens.

Anyone can have a good disposition when all is calm and serene, but what about when you are in a whirl, and things go wrong, or you don't feel very well? God can give you a steady disposition. Ask Him.

Growing in Maturity

How can you close the gap between God's standard of what you should be and what you are? You know what you *ought* to be but *how* do you get there? Here are a few steps that have helped many women:

1. *Be honest with God.* Identify your need, your weakness or your sin (1 John 1:9). Not saying, "I don't love him," but saying honestly "I can't stand him, Father, forgive me."

2. *Confess* your bitterness, putting into words the way you feel you were treated (Hebrews 12: 15). "You *know* how he judges and he had no business asking me. I just *hate* it when he's so nosey. I *do* resent him, Lord; please forgive me and cleanse my heart."

3. *Choose* to forgive each offender and his offense (Matthew 6:12). "All right, I forgive him, Lord."

4. *Accept* and thank God for the cleansing from your sin (1 John 1:9). "Thank You that You forgive me and cleanse my heart with Your blood. By the indwelling of Your Holy Spirit I *can* change."

5. *Ask* God to fill you with His love (1 John 4:8). "I know You love him. Please let Your love flow from me."

6. *Thank* God for His *power* to love (Mark 9:23). "Thank You, heavenly Father, for the power to love."

7. Now, *live* in the confidence of what God has done for you!

There are no "pat" answers. There is no easy solution. In the end God holds the key. He loves you and has your best interests at heart. If you are having problems finding the answer, remember, you are His child. He won't bow to your terms. You have to accept and comply with *His* way. Also remember, His way is directed by His perfect love and compassion for you.

It's so easy to rationalize or minimize the wrong. Often this is not done deliberately, but we are blind until God opens our eyes. He will give us insight when we really *want* to see and ask Him to meet our needs and make His way clear.

With God there are no wishy-washy standards of right or wrong. He not only expects us to be holy as He is holy (1 Peter 1:15), but He provides the power for the holy life He expects. The Holy Spirit who lives in all true believers enables us to do what God requires (Luke 11:13).

It's so easy for women to live by their emotions. We have done it for so long that it is a habit. Living by our will has to be developed in us. If, a couple of days after God has filled your heart with love for your husband, you wake up with a headache and don't *feel* loving, don't panic. Nothing has changed, only your feelings. You can expect them to change, especially if this is your 28th day! But God has not taken away His gift of love.

Or, just when you begin to feel that benevolent glow, your husband does some aggravating thing which fills you with irritation — don't panic. God is "stretching" your capacity to love. It doesn't have to end the minute you get mad. Love has to learn *how* to suffer long, longer and longer, before it has any real stability. Accept these tests as God's opportunity to enlarge your capacity. As you demonstrate your love by loving deeds and a loving attitude, you will be amazed to find the *feeling of love* returns.

I have spent a good bit of time in this section because I feel that we find the heart of spiritual maturity in a life changed by God.

It Is Safe to Fail

In the end it is God who makes the truly mature woman, and He's been in the business for years! He will use the circumstances of your life to mold you into the godly woman He has created you to become. Pain, suffering, difficulty and loss are as much His tools as joy, prosperity and ease.

Learn to trust God when you fail. Remember, *God never fails.* As you yield yourself, He will use your failures to build a deeper faith, added strength, insight and compassion. Later He will use you to share with others the breadth and depth of His perfect love in suffering.

> "For this reason . . . I bow my knees before the Father. . . . May He grant you out of the rich treasury of His glory to be strengthened *and* reinforced with mighty power in the inner man. . . . May Christ through your faith . . . dwell . . . in your hearts! May you be rooted deep in love *and* founded securely on love, that you may have the power *and* be strong to apprehend . . . with all the saints . . . what is the breadth and length and height and depth [of it]; . . . to know — practically, through experience for yourselves — the love of Christ, which far surpasses mere knowledge (without experience); that you may . . . have the richest measure of the divine Presence and become a body wholly filled and flooded with God Himself" (Ephesians 3:14-19, *Amplified*).

Chapter Five

Emotional Maturity

Questions to Ask Yourself

— What qualities of emotional maturity do you need to develop?

— What command or encouragement did you read in your Bible today?

— What change of attitude or action has your Bible reading led to?

— How do you accept reverses?

— How do you react to criticism? How will you change?

— What kind of atmosphere does your presence create in your home? In what way can you improve it?

6
Happy Homemaking

Fun and Freedom

Are you fun to live with? Is homemaking a chore or a challenge? Have you mastered the art of living with today's stress?

Life today is a far cry from the relaxed life of fifty years ago, or even twenty years ago. Many women are unprepared to cope with urbanization and the stress of living in this "space whirl."

There used to be time to think — at least when you drove the horse and buggy to church! Today you are rushed from home, to school, to church, to the club, and back home to throw a TV dinner into the oven. Children ask for help with homework, your husband wants you to go out with him and tonight the church has its monthly women's meeting. *Which* do you do? The pressure of demands is crushing.

How can you stay liberated and full of fun with all of these pressures? How can you be an adequate wife and mother with such a schedule?

There are no easy, instant solutions, but perhaps some suggestions could help you think toward a solution in your own busy whirl! I would suggest that you take a little time away from home. Perhaps you could go to a park, or for a drive to some restful spot or even to a corner of the public library and turn your back to the room and shut yourself away for a few minutes of quietness. If you can't get away, retreating to the bathroom behind a locked door is sometimes a solution to a few minutes for creative reflection!

Try first to identify the source of your stress. Is it actually the circumstances in which you are caught or is it your *attitude* to the circumstances of your busy life which is bothering you? Is it realistic to carry such a load and to be involved in so many activities?

Think of different women you know. It could help you to be more objective in your situation if you take into account *their* situations, *their* responsibilities. Why do some women seem relaxed and a joy to visit while others make you feel tense and almost like an intruder?

Betty and Marjorie are friends of mine. It is a study to observe their lives. Betty is always under pressure. Marjorie is usually relaxed.

Betty has two older children and a small house requiring little work. Although it is always neat, I'm made aware of all the work it takes to keep a family of four in a clean house — to keep up with the washing and ironing and to participate in church activities. Since living is such a burden to Betty, you hesitate to ask her to do anything else. She tells me she never has any time for herself or the things *she* wants to do. Betty does all her work with a heavy spirit. There is never any letup for her. As she finishes one job she is dreading the next!

Marjorie has five children. Their home is small, but, being old, more difficult to keep looking clean and neat. There are some days when things are scattered around, but if you visit her another time, the house is tidy and Marjorie may be drinking coffee and chatting leisurely with a neighbor. Marjorie finds time to participate in school and church activities. Currently she is working on a personal improvement course.

What makes the difference in the two women? True, part of it is temperament, but notice the difference in their attitudes. Now, evaluate your situation. Take a deep, deep breath. Let it out slowly. Relax. Now, in the quietness of your soul ask your loving heavenly Father to enable you to do some straight thinking. What is your *attitude* to what you have to do . . . ?

What activity seems to unbalance the running of your home? Perhaps you can cope with the regular activities, but each Tuesday evening when you go bowling, the household is all upset, or, every Thursday, when you join the neighbors for a coffee klatsch, you lose a morning and take two days to catch up! Is it your attitude toward these activities, or should you really drop one of them? One less activity might help you cope better with your current family demands.

It is hard not to compare yourself unfavorably with other women. But if you do, you must take into account *all* their circumstances. For example, I felt so frustrated because I couldn't manage to be as free as a friend of mine. She could participate in more activities outside of her home than I could. Later I realized her husband's needs could be met differently than mine. Having fewer and older children in her household made a big difference too. You cannot compare yourself and your limitations to anyone else. Your situation is uniquely yours. You need to accept your total situation and adjust your activities to provide a relaxed atmosphere in your home.

There are times when pressure can be used as a friend. It stretches your capacity and can be a challenge to find inner peace during stress and a better way to cope with a situation you cannot change.

At other times pressure can be an enemy. Too many extraneous activities keep your life in a continual whirl, with no time to think, meditate or collect your inner resources to organize your time. You become like the frantic woman, who, unsure of her direction, doubles her speed! How often have you been racing madly ahead with no real goal and asking God to bless you!

Think again. Are you creating your ideal of what a home should be like? Is it your husband's dream home? What elements make an ideal home in which all the members can find peace and refuge? List them.

This is probably enough to think about for one time. Mull over these questions in the back of your mind as you return to your home duties. You may even find this short time alone has lifted your spirit, thrown a little light on your way and restored a zest for homemaking.

Evaluate Your Schedule

On another day take out your notebook and begin to list all of your activities. Evaluate each in the light of your major responsibilities. Try to be realistic about the *amount of time* each of these activities takes — such as cooking, washing, ironing, shopping and church. Travel is time-consuming too. Even when an activity only takes an hour in the morning, getting ready to go, and socializing with your friend afterward can use up a whole morning. Can you participate in all these activities and still be the relaxed wife and mother your husband and children need?

Life today is full. You will have to determine, with God's help, the priorities for your own use of time. Pressure is lifted when there is an inner assurance that you are doing what is *right for you* — not what *you think* others may expect of you, but what *you know* you can handle in your situation.

You will find that each year your activities will change and your capacity will grow. When your children are small don't expect to do what a woman does whose children are grown.

Learning to live freely within the scope of your temperament and that of your husband brings peace and happiness. Husbands differ widely in outlook. One man may want his wife home in the evening while another may be glad for time alone with the children and happy that his wife can enjoy an evening out with her friends. It is wonderful to be free from the feeling of guilt and frustration that many have because they cannot tailor their life to that of another couple's.

Disliking Housework

"I never was cut out for housework," Cynthia moaned bitterly as she once again faced the chaos of her little house and the work of bringing order to it before her husband returned home from work. Later she asked a friend how a woman could actually *enjoy* the *chore* of housework!

"Really, Cindy, it's all in the way you look at it. Are you keeping house or making a home?" Then the friend went on to share the thrill of finding God's way for her in becoming a happy home-maker. She encouraged Cynthia to take pride in running a home that pleased her husband, a home to which he'd eagerly look forward to returning after a hard day's work.

What a challenge to plan your work and then work your plan. Fifteen minutes of planning your day can save hours of wasted motion and aimlessness. It's thrilling to see how skilled you can become in managing the details of your home. But if you underestimate your time and a meal is late, don't be discouraged — start earlier tomorrow.

Do you find you have a particular time of stress or a particular hour of the day when you are easily irritated with the children? Proverbs 22:3 has some good advice for you: "A prudent woman (man) seeth the evil and hideth herself." In other words a wise woman knows what's coming and prepares for it. Does a member of the family whirl into the house in such a way he throws everyone into confusion? What should you do in order to cope with this situation? How can you prepare yourself? Sometimes anticipating the situation conditions your mind for what's coming and enables you to accept with inner quiet what could be a time of tension.

You can learn so much from your friends. Nearly every woman has learned ways of handling tensions or shortcuts in housekeeping. Some women have a store of delicious, quickie-meal ideas. There are many books you can read that make housekeeping fun and a challenge. I've profited from the following:

Meals in Minutes by the Better Homes and Gardens Editors.

The I Hate to Housekeep Book by Peg Bracken.

Management in the Home by Lillian Gilbreth *et al.*

A Woman in Her Home by Ella May Miller.

The Working Wives Cook Book by Theodora Zavin and Freda Stuart.

There are two ways to view housework — negatively and positively. Perhaps one negative aspect of housework is that you feel it cannot be measured. You think a working person knows by the amount of work turned out whether or not he has had a good day. There seems, however, to be no standard of measurement for the home. If today you cleaned half the house thoroughly could you have done more? If you sewed today, should you have washed instead? It is even more disconcerting to feel a whole day has passed with nothing but interruptions and nothing done you had planned. At the end of such a frustrating day, it is hard to greet your husband cheerfully and be ready for the children's return from school. But some days this cannot be avoided and is just par for the course.

Now looking positively at homemaking we see it provides a tremendous scope for creativity and experimentation. No two days are alike. How can you organize your work and use your time and strength to the best advantage? How can you work into your day or week something you consider a treat such as painting, writing, a day out with friends, reading, or redecorating a room?

Unpleasant Tasks

"Whatsoever thy hand findeth to do, do it with thy might!"   (Ecclesiastes 9:10)

Everyone prefers one area of work to another. Don't spend time dreading the ironing, do it first! Then reward yourself . . . perhaps with a coffee break? Really, it's great to see God give you an enthusiasm for work you would not naturally enjoy. I used to hate ironing. But as I began to perfect it and raced against my own time, it became fun. Later I realized it was an ideal time to pray for the person whose clothes I was ironing.

Lately, I have come to enjoy going through closets, sorting toys, cleaning out cluttered corners and giving things away. An outgrown coat brought much delight to a small girl's heart and saved her parents the expense of a new one.

The most fun of all can come after you have tidied up the basement closet. One lovely weekend your husband heads for the closet to get his fishing gear. He steadies himself for the avalanche of skates, coats, golf clubs and sleeping bags, opens the door cautiously, looks in, opens it wider — his face is a picture of startled unbelief!

Gracious Hospitality

Mrs. Baxter, referred to in chapter one, exemplified graciousness. Everyone seemed to blossom in the delightful atmosphere of her home. After we came to know the family, the older daughter laughingly said in front of her mother, "We love having company, then we know we *have* to clean house." Mrs. Baxter laughed and added, "There seem to be so many other things more important, some things that take so much time, that we can only keep the house in order until we have company! Of course we have to make a good impression then!" It didn't take me long to find out that they had a constant stream of company, for the family kept open house and exhibited a real spirit of hospitality.

Entertaining

My cousin Jean does a lot of entertaining. Before her guests sit down to dinner, she runs a sink full of hot water. As she serves her food the pots go right into the dishpan. Then, between the first and the second course, it takes her only a few minutes to wash the dinner plates. Guests chatting happily in a relaxed atmosphere do not notice her absence. Women are amazed that at the end of the meal only the dessert dishes need to be washed.

Jean's husband is so proud of her. He told me how neighbors can count on her in times of need. Their home is always open.

Her husband can bring home unexpected guests any time. She *keeps* the house tidy, rather than having to tidy it up when company is expected! And she is just as gracious to the "way-out" young person as she is to Bob's boss or secretary.

Money Management

What can bring more joy or cause more sorrow than money, particularly its management? How you handle money depends on your sense of values and it's unusual for a husband and wife to begin marriage with the *same* values. Often it takes time to work out a budget agreeable to both. Try to understand your husband's point of view and take your time about suggesting changes.

One woman I knew came from a well-to-do background, but her husband came from poverty. Their income was small but adequate. However, she had to

104

account for nearly every penny she spent for the first five years of their marriage. Through the wife's prayers her husband was convicted of his lack of trust. He saw how well his wife handled their finances, and was freed from his earlier qualms about her ability to spend their money wisely.

Another wife was able to save her husband from serious financial reverses by living frugally. Betty believed in a savings account and planning ahead. Her husband felt that any leftover money should be used for fun. In time he accepted Betty's way and how thankful they were for their savings when the husband was out of work.

The Bible clearly teaches that the first tenth of our income belongs to God (Malachi 3:8-10). These verses describe the blessings that will be poured out upon those who put God first in this practical way. It is easy to say we love God with all our hearts, but where we put our treasure our hearts will follow. Money is the "acid test." In this materialistic world it is easy to be enticed into spending more and more for luxuries, and less and less for promoting the kingdom of God. It's exciting to see the need of missionaries, radio work, orphanages, or an organizational outreach and be able to fill the need with money the Lord has entrusted to us. A husband has to concentrate on his job. Many times the wife has more opportunity to be aware of needs. With the right attitude and prayer for wisdom she can do much to help her husband be aware of the needs of others.

Another interesting Biblical passage on finances speaks to us as responsible parents. "The children ought not to lay up for the parents, but the parents for the children" (2 Corinthians 12:14). Wives need to work out a sensible savings plan (for both long- and short-range savings) with their husbands. You need to start the habit of tithing and saving even on a small income. With more money comes more responsibility, so unless tithing is a settled principle, it becomes harder and harder to start.

Children

Marjorie resented her children because they kept her from the things she enjoyed doing more than washing diapers and picking up toys.

Lydia eagerly looked forward to children as the culmination of her love for her husband and the fulfillment of her joys of being a wife. She was excited with the thought of training children to live effectively in their generation.

What is your attitude toward your children? Are they God's precious gift of life to you and your husband? Do you anticipate the responsibility of seeing these children blossom in your home to fulfill the purpose of God in giving them to you? Will your children rise up and call you blessed (Proverbs 31:28)? Will they appreciate what you have taken time to build into their lives? What will your children say about your daily attitudes — hearing what you say, watching what you do? Are you communicating to them the depth of God's love and yours?

Some houses are so spotless neither the children nor the husband feels at home. Others are so untidy the husband and children are ashamed to bring their friends home. What is the happy balance for *your* home?

A woman with three or four young children cannot have the house as orderly as the woman whose children are all in school. One wife with little ones found that if she could pick up the toys in the front hall her husband could accept the rest of the house being untidy. That one little problem caused real conflict and hurt feelings *until the wife put herself into his place* and saw how the house looked to him as he stumbled over the heap of toys in the front hall. After she realized this, it seemed a small task to please him by picking up the toys in the front hall.

A loving attitude creates freedom and happiness in a home. Seeking the best for the children is a constant goal.

Camille's love of training her children and *the happy attitude she cultivated toward housework* (even though there were some things she didn't like to do) rubbed off on her children. They developed an attitude of cooperation and household jobs were done cheerfully since this became the family's accepted way of life.

It is of tremendous importance to build into children a respect for their father. Children will reflect their mother's attitude to him. There are times when a father shows his worst side at home, but a mother can do much to put him in a good light and draw out his best side toward the children. Most fathers will rise to their best before the children when they realize how important it is.

In a happy home, differences of opinion are wholesome and healthy discussions are viewed as good mental exercise. *Arguments* should be in private! At a "table debate" the children should not be asked to take sides, because they cannot help but be emotionally torn between their parents in a heated argument.

A husband can relax and be at peace when he knows that his wife has the right attitude toward their children. Everyone makes mistakes, but many of these can be covered by strong, unselfish love — and children know when you really care and are concerned for *their* very best. A husband can also be at rest if you both set goals for your children's character development. Respect, obedience, responsibility and confidence in God are qualities you should seek to develop in your children.

Another way to help your children is to plan time to read to them. Books can be selected to help them build a value system. There are many uplifting, character-building stories, including novels and biographies of famous people and missionaries, with which to stimulate their desire for high ideals.

There are two excellent books I have found helpful; one provides a guide in character building and the other helps in choosing reading material for children:

Your Child by Dr. Anna Mow.
Honey for a Child's Heart by Gladys Hunt.

Chapter Six

Happy Homemaking

Questions to Ask Yourself

— What can you do to improve your schedule?
— What unpleasant job that you tend to put off will you try to do this week?
— What new touch will you give to the home, or what delectable dish will you prepare for your husband as a surprise-of-love?
— What have you thought of doing for someone that you keep putting off? (Write it down and do it!)
— Does your budget need rethinking? Are you making the best possible use of your income: Too many time payments? Living too close to the edge? Wasteful spending? Does your handling of money please God?
— What is a better way to train your children in obedience, respect, self-control, responsibility and confidence in God?
— How can you help the children to see the best in your husband even when he is tired and crabby?
— What books have you purchased for yourself and the children?
— What books should you buy?

Part Three:

Understanding Your Problems

7

Winning Your Husband to Christ

Merle's Victory

As Merle started supper, Jim went out to mow the lawn. Seconds later the back door flew open and Jim stood there enraged.

"Why didn't you get gas for the mower the last time you had the car? You knew the tin was empty. Why don't you look after things around here? The least you could do is see to the gas. You expect me to do everything. All you do is sit around gabbing with your friends . . . if you'd *do* something once in awhile. . . ."

Furious anger and hatred flared up in Merle. Another one of Jim's unfair accusations! Bitter words poured into her mind. Her mouth opened. "Now, God!" she prayed and closed her lips. *This is it,* she thought. *What she had faced and decided to do in Jim's absence, must be put into practice now, in his presence.* Instantly she prayed for love as she confessed her anger and resentment to God.

Jim slammed through the kitchen into the living room. He threw himself into a big chair storming abusively all the while.

God, You love Jim, Merle prayed. *Fill me with Your love for him now!*

As Jim ranted on, Merle walked into the living room. Jim glared. Merle looked into his anger-filled eyes and said softly, with deep sincerity, "I love you, Jim." Jim was staggered. Where was the defensive ugliness from Merle which made his violence more justifiable? It was as though the walls of the room were crumbling.

Thus began Merle's creative, positive demonstration of God's way to live in the home. This

111

was the end of fighting back, the end of nagging.

She memorized First Peter 3 and Ephesians 5: 22-24. Prayer became the first as well as the last resort.

Merle prayed in times of crisis. She prayed while doing housework. The task of homemaking became filled with love. Ironing became a time she could pray for Jim and ask the Lord to fill her heart with love for him. Cooking became a means of pleasing her husband.

Now, God-given concern for Jim enabled Merle to stand in her husband's shoes and "tune in" to his outlook on life.

- What made him feel as he did?
  - What kind of love and understanding did he need?
    - What made him suffer?
      - What made him happy?
        - What encouraged him?

A God-worked submission began to follow in every area of her life. Jim saw Merle's change. He saw her active dependence upon him. He saw his responsibility for "their" actions, which drove him to find God. This made a man of him.

In time he submitted to God as Merle had submitted to him. As Jim began to love Merle with Christ's love, "submission" melted in that love. Merle was free. She no longer had to account for everything — she was free to use the car and the checkbook.

Through submission Merle had proved herself a worthy wife, willing to please her husband. She ceased to be a competitor, and became a trusted companion.

Jim's attitudes also began to change. He became considerate of his wife. Merle thanks God that Jim did not yield to her former self-centered and childish behavior. She saw how unlovely she had been. God worked a change in her to His glory.

Even their sex life became meaningful as each became concerned for the happiness of the other.

Neither Jim nor Merle were Christians when they married. Some time afterward Merle realized her need for a Savior. As she grew in her Christian life, she saw her need to adapt to Jim's way of life. In time this brought about Jim's salvation. Merle shudders to think of the results had she continued to dig in her heels and fight back. The freedom she fought for did not come until she relinquished it and accepted all that real heart submission means — yielding her rights to herself in the confidence that she could trust herself to God and trust God to work in her husband's life.

What is your situation? Has your love for your husband grown through the years? Are you closer? Are you more understanding? Has your Christianity separated you from your husband so you no longer share the same pleasures? Do you display a desire to meet his needs and share his interests? What about friends? How do you treat his in comparison to your own Christian friends?

God's Plan

God has a plan for the winning of your husband to Himself. In First Peter 2:9 God says, "Ye are a chosen generation . . . that ye should show forth the praises of him who hath called you out of darkness into his marvelous light."

Then this passage goes on to show how this is done. You are to abstain from lust, be honest, submit to those in authority and fear God. Servants are to submit to their masters. Children are to submit to their parents. Christ, our example, submitted to the will of God. Now in First Peter 3:1, God says, "Likewise" — in the same way, with the same attitude — wives are to submit to their husbands. Submission is an attitude of heart. It is not so much *what* you do, but the attitude in which you

113

do what is right. Submission includes adapting to your husband with love, insight, and empathy. Remember, he is the one responsible to God for your home. God's instructions to him are to love his wife with the same tender love Christ has for His bride, the church (Ephesians 5:25).

How to Win Your Husband

God's way is positive and creative, *never nagging*. It challenges and demands all that a woman has — both spiritually and mentally. The *way,* followed clearly, simply and in faith, is bound to bring results. Very little worth having is easily obtained. Many say that our salvation is free, but it cost Jesus much suffering — it cost Him His life. Just to live the Christian life takes all the resources of patience, love, insight, understanding and the sensitivity God has given.

It is thrilling that the Bible gives clear instructions to women whose husbands do not believe in Christ:

> "In the same way you wives must submit [adapt] yourselves to your husbands, so that if some of them do not believe God's Word, *they will be won over to believe by your conduct.* It will not be necessary for you to say a word, for they will see how pure and reverent your conduct is. You should not use outward aids to make yourselves beautiful, as in the way you fix your hair, or in the jewelry you put on, or the dresses you wear. Instead, your beauty should consist of your true inner self, the ageless beauty of a *gentle and quiet spirit,* which is of *great value* in God's sight. For this is the way the devout women of the past, who hoped in God, used to make themselves beautiful; they submitted themselves to their husbands. Sarah was like that; she obeyed Abraham and called him 'My master.' You are now her daughters if you do good and are not afraid of anything" (1 Peter 3:1-6, *Good News for Modern Man*).

This passage needs a lot of thought for its full meaning and depth to be comprehended. In today's hurried, skim-the-surface existence little time is taken for thinking and meditation. Effective businessmen eat, drink and sleep creative ideas in order to make a success of their work.

Can you do less to make a success of your marriage? Scripture gives the God-given principle for success — submission (1 Peter 3). Submission includes three facets of a woman's life:

- her conduct
- her grooming
- her faith.

How is your conduct in the home? Are you a joy to live with? It is easy to be nice to people outside the home, but what is your attitude toward your husband? Your children? Do you give them the love and the consideration you would give a guest?

Gracious Conduct

A friend of mine had a husband who was not a Christian. She was greatly concerned for her husband and hoped that if I were ever in her town I would visit in her home. Some weeks later I was visiting friends nearby, so I phoned to confirm her invitation. Her husband told me his wife was away, but he was sure she would like me to have dinner with them that evening, and he would pick me up.

The husband was very gracious as he drove me to their home, and we arrived, to my surprise, five minutes ahead of his wife. *What about dinner,* I thought, since she had been away all day. The wife arrived, greeted me warmly, and we followed her to the kitchen.

With boyish pride her husband opened the oven door to show his wife the dinner he had prepared in her absence!

Without a word of appreciation the wife snapped, "Why did you fix the potatoes *that* way?" He said nothing and walked out of the kitchen. The dinner was delicious, but table talk was difficult. The wife tried to talk about faith in Christ. The husband was a perfect gentleman, but I had no heart left to tell of my Lord who wins the respect of husbands by the loving, gracious conduct of their wives.

What is your attitude to your husband? Do people see your respect for him? Contrast the woman who, at a church supper, made derogatory comments about the amount of food her husband had heaped on his plate with the wife whose eyes always glowed and whose voice softened when she spoke of her husband's encouragement, ability and fine character.

What is your attitude to homemaking? Do you delight in keeping a lovely home that will be a credit to your husband? Have you trained your children to respect their father? What is your reputation in the church and in the community? Do you worry, fret and lose your temper, or are you finding the answer to these problems?

Outward Beauty

Many women depend on their outward beauty and cultivated charm to win their way. God doesn't despise attention given to personal attractiveness for the Bible refers to a woman's care of herself in the Song of Solomon as well as in Proverbs 31. God does have much to say about laziness. It is inexcusable for a woman to be untidy or sloppy in her appearance. God loves beauty and cleanliness. But God also makes it clear that we are not to rely upon this. It's delightful to see a woman who has done all she can to make herself attractive by using becoming colors and clothes best suited to her, but her real charm comes from the inner beauty of a meek and quiet spirit.

Study yourself. Is there anything that could make you more appealing to your husband? Being too busy is no excuse for not keeping yourself attractive. You owe it to your husband and to your own self-respect. How do you look at the beginning and at the end of the day? What is the image your husband carries in his heart as he leaves for work in the morning and as he returns home in the evening? It takes effort to lose ten pounds or to set your hair each night, but oh, the worthwhileness of it all!

Once I stayed in an apartment building where the other women were very friendly. We often had coffee and chatted together. But at four o'clock one of the women would excuse herself and dash home to shower, change, straighten the house and put her baby into a clean dress. At five-thirty this wife, looking sweet and fresh, would be preparing supper when her husband came home. I guessed they'd been married about a year and a half, which seemed a long time to continue such care and attention for her husband. Out of curiosity I asked her how long she had been married. "Seven years," she said happily!

Inward Beauty

When Fred and I were first married we lived with Ellie and Ben. It was a joy to live in the atmosphere of love and graciousness which pervaded their home. Their marriage had not always been that way, they assured us. They married with Christian ideals. Ben, a naturally gentle man, saw his need to be lovingly firm. In answer to prayer, Ellie changed from a naturally domineering woman to a gentle and submissive one.

One day Fred and Ben were going to attend a men's meeting at church. I was helping Ellie in the kitchen as the men came through on their way to the meeting. Fred, as always, was dressed neatly. Ben was clean, but he looked like he'd slept in his sport coat.

117

"Are you wearing *that* jacket to the meeting?" questioned Ellie, gently. I looked quickly to see if he resented the implication.

"Yes, I am," he answered with quiet firmness but no hint of resentment, and walked out the door. I quickly glanced to her to see if his appearance would make her angry. Smiling and unruffled she turned to me and we continued our work.

If that had been *my* husband . . . !

Only God could have worked this meek and quiet inner beauty. God can create meekness and humility in a proud woman. What are your areas of pride? Will you entrust your husband to God? Will you leave the consequences of his actions with Him? Will you let God create a quiet spirit of trust in you?

Why is a meek and quiet spirit of such great price in the sight of God? Because *real* humility is not natural to any of us. It can come only through deep trust and confidence in a loving God during difficult and trying circumstances—producing great strength under control.

Faith at Work

What is your attitude toward God? Is your conduct one of deep reverence toward Him and His standards for your life? Does your husband see a real love for God and His Word or does he see that church bores you and that you seldom read the Bible with pleasure? Does he see, when you pray, that God answers?

As you obey God in practical loving ways, God will work for you as He did for Merle. It was not easy for Merle to be a loving wife, but day after day, as she spent time with God, she prayed about how to be to Jim what he needed. *She talked less and less to Jim about God, but talked more and more to God about Jim.*

There is so much involved in an attitude of reverence toward God. Resentment, bitterness and an unforgiving spirit cannot continue. Do you harbor buried resentments from past injuries? Is there an unforgiving spirit for real or imagined hurts? All of these attitudes can cause a rankle in your spirit and hinder the work of God. Forgiving your husband does not make his wrong right, but it does clear the way for God to work. The flow of God's love through you is hindered by a life filled with the sin of wrong attitudes. Are there areas for which you need to ask forgiveness? Have you been critical or unappreciative, cold or accusing? Sin causes fermentation which later bubbles up into anger and frustration.

For God to alter your attitudes, you first need His cleaning from wrong attitudes and actions. Then you need the infilling of God's Spirit of love, and finally you need to ask your husband's forgiveness for your wrong attitudes and actions. As you respect and obey the laws of God's love, He will begin His transforming work in your home.

Godly Confidence

Think of the trust Sarah had to have when her husband Abraham told the king of Egypt that she was his sister — a half-truth. It's not without reason that when God asks the woman to submit to man, He also tells her not to be afraid (1 Peter 3:6). God knows all about demanding, unreasonable husbands. His way is to show us His miracle-working power. As we demonstrate a confidence in God that produces an unshakable, quiet spirit before our husbands, He continues His work in them.

However, some husbands become more demanding and unreasonable as they resist turning their lives over to God. This is a time of suffering for many a wife. Only an abiding, steady trust in God can sustain her through these trying days, weeks, months and sometimes years. Maintain a spirit of prayer for your husband as you try to think understandingly of him. His life is not easy, especially not now, since added to his daily grind is his inner struggle. Are you able to stay positive toward him?

- Expect God to work in your situation.
  - Wait expectantly.
    - He will not fail.

Chapter Seven

Winning Your Husband to Christ

Questions to Ask Yourself

— In what ways has becoming a Christian made you a better wife?
— How could you be more winsome to your husband?
— What are "spiritual" sore points in your marriage? What do you *expect* God to do about them?
— What can you do to win your husband to Christ?
— What Christian books could you leave around the house that would be of interest to your husband?
— What friends could you invite over — friends whose husbands were much like yours before they became Christians?
— What places could you take your husband so that he can hear speakers that would interest *him*?
— How can your homemaking be more to his liking?

8
Problems Women Face

Of the many problems women face in marriage, I have tried to select those which have been brought to me most often. The answers could provide the key to something you are facing. Perhaps these same principles could apply to your problem.

Absentee Husband

Many husbands have jobs that require a great deal of travel. Their wives may find it difficult to adjust to being alone so often. Yet this may be the type of life your husband feels is right for him and enjoys the most. Loneliness, boredom, frustration with the children and decision-making without your husband can be overwhelming. If your husband's work keeps him away from home much of the time, you will have to accept and adjust to his absence creatively for your husband's well-being and for your own happiness. This may be hard, but it is important.

Bring this problem to God and ask Him to free you from any self-pity and to show you how to build a satisfying life with the children. You have an exciting opportunity to develop other interests, such as art, reading, a course at night or correspondence school. You could take up new activities . . . one day a week as a volunteer in a hospital or church would be a worthwhile change. Then plan carefully for the little time your husband is home. An alert, growing and happy wife with a wholesome outlook toward her position in life will do more to bring her husband home as often as possible than a complaining, unhappy one. Like the oyster, build a beautiful pearl around what could be a wretched irritant.

Paul had to be away from home much of the time. This was a source of great irritation to Virginia. She nagged him so that he began to stay away more than necessary. One evening he even "forgot" his birthday dinner. He called his wife to say he was eating supper with a friend. Virginia was so furious she threw the whole delicious dinner into the garbage uneaten.

Through the testimony of a woman who moved into her town, she was challenged to look to God to make her the woman her husband would *want* to return to. She acknowledged her bitterness, confessed it to God and forgave her husband for not coming home. She began working on being attractive and having things the way Paul liked them. Their home life was transformed.

One evening she shared the story of her changed attitude with some women at a friend's home while her husband was away on a trip. With glowing face, she said, "I couldn't have come tomorrow night, because Paul is coming home and I'll be waiting for him." When she finished speaking the phone rang. It was Paul. He had driven all night just to be home a day earlier!

Interrupted Schedules

Some wives find it difficult to drop what they are doing to do something unexpected with their husbands. Are you rigid? Are you adaptable only when the situation suits you, or the event is to your liking? It's not always convenient to drop your home duties when your husband asks you to go with him. But this is *very important*. Often it is a sacrifice. To catch up with your neglected work means late hours, rushing through work or reshuffling an already full schedule. But you will find that these are the times your husband really needs you. He may need to talk to you, or just want to

122

know you care and that he is important to you — more important than your schedule.

Claudia's husband begged her to go with him on some of his longer trips. He hated to be alone. Occasionally she went, but her heart was not with him — she pined for the children. Jim needed his wife. Her letters or even her half-hearted presence were not enough — he needed *her*. The children were well provided for, but Claudia put them before her husband and seemed blind to his need. In his loneliness Jim found another woman who gave him all her attention. Today, Claudia has her children — but not for long. Soon, the last child will be out of the nest, and Claudia will be alone.

The schedule of a doctor-husband can present other difficulties. Plans are often made with friends on his evening off only to have him called away for an emergency. Interrupted evenings are almost routine for a friend of mine whose husband is a surgeon. He will not even leave on their vacation if he has a patient in critical condition, although another doctor might more than adequately take over. Some wives resent this and can't or won't accept their husband's long hours. However, unless you mentally and emotionally set your husband free and plan enthusiastically for the times he *is* home, he may find it easier to stay away even more. Who wants to come home to a woman filled with resentment whether spoken or stifled?

You may have a legitimate complaint. But put yourself in his place. Think of *his* feelings and responsibility. Remember that the responsibility of life and death weighs heavily upon him. Ask God to open your husband's heart to a change of pace. Then, when you mention how you feel about his spending so little time at home, he may see the family's need for his precious time and do his best to adjust his working hours.

Perhaps your husband changes jobs too frequently. You are afraid he will *never* settle down. You know no job is perfect and feel he is just chasing the pot of gold at the foot of the rainbow. But is he? Perhaps he has not yet found an outlet for his creative talent.

Ask God where your husband fits. If he is creative, encourage him to look for a creative job; if he is a leader, to look for work where there is opportunity for leadership.

There are husbands who want to try some new occupation more suited to their abilities, but this sort of uncertainty can strike terror to a wife's heart. Her fears can dim her husband's courage to seek a more suitable career.

> Bill dearly loved mechanics, but he married young and did not have the required training. Year after year passed in a job he hated. He tried tinkering in his garage. His job was secure, but paid so poorly that he had to work long hours to provide adequately for his family. His wife Betty has a keen mind and a thirst for knowledge. As her husband failed to challenge her mentally, she felt she had to go to school or wither away.
>
> "What are you taking in college?" I asked.
>
> "Hebrew," was her enthusiastic reply. "I find it so challenging."
>
> I talked to Betty about encouraging her husband to go to school by making some temporary sacrifice, perhaps working herself to free Bill to develop his skills. Betty could not see any sense in my suggestion nor Bill's frustration. She felt he was doing all right and *ought* to be happy in his job. Besides, cutting down on his hours, while he built up the trade he really liked seemed too risky to her.

Salary is not always the most important criterion for a job. Your husband needs the freedom to find the job which will meet his own need as well as provide for the needs of his family.

Certainly, *there are* risks involved, but remember, you do not step out alone. God is with you. Your husband's happiness and the development of his potential are far more important than any risks.

Potential

A wife can hinder a husband from reaching his potential whether it is for some occupation he enjoys, some hobby he likes, or for an education he needs. Just because what he wants to do doesn't appeal to her, or feels it's a waste of money and effort, doesn't mean a wife should squelch his desire to pursue something different or special. Every man has hidden depths, hidden possibilities. Some are obvious, others less so, but they are nonetheless real. A wife's encouragement can do much to bring them to the surface.

Susan had developed a mental block because of a situation she had encountered as a young person which she was afraid would be repeated in her own life.

Bob had not finished college. After fifteen years of marriage, he felt his need for more education. Although Susan was a college graduate, she was afraid to have her husband return to school.

"I have seen too many wives left behind mentally and then their husbands lose interest in them," she remarked fearfully.

"You don't have to worry, Susan," I sought to reassure her. "Marriage breakdowns come for other reasons — not minor educational differences. Discouraging him is more apt to drive you apart. Your *encouragement* at this time should actually draw you closer to each other."

If your husband has the desire to accomplish a task, he no doubt has the ability. He has to start somewhere. Both of you are responsible for developing his God-

125

given gifts. You'll be amazed what your support and confidence will do with hidden potential when you strengthen and encourage your husband in a new undertaking. Mental and spiritual stimulus can be developed through the way he spends his free time on a hobby.

Although Sam enjoyed his work with people, at home he was a radio and electronics fan. There were nights when Ann was a "short-wave widow," but she encouraged Sam's hobby and never complained. Instead she cultivated interests she could do alone. Little did Ann realize that the day would come when Sam would lose his "secure" job and be able to turn to electronics and engineering for work . . . and at double his former salary!

Realistic Potential

A man can trust the wife who does not *overestimate* him. She needs to seek the balance between what she *thinks* her husband can do, and what he *really* can do successfully, comfortably, and happily.

Perhaps there is something you think your husband should do but he doesn't agree. Beware of the subtle danger of comparing your husband with "Mr. Jones" rather than seeing him as he is.

Charlotte's husband began to advance in his work. The added income and prestige was an incentive to push ahead faster. One day Charlotte realized that subconsciously money and prestige were about to take precedent over Frank's happiness, ability and potential. When Charlotte discovered that her *false values* would force Frank into a position he didn't want, she stopped pushing him. She realized that his happiness was more important than becoming president of the company! "I'm perfectly happy, if you are," Charlotte assured him. Her new attitude set Frank free. She saw the importance of his values. Then he was able to open his heart to her. He felt more comfortable in a position with fewer demands on his time that left him free to spend more time with his family. Together they concluded that this was more important to them than the prestige of status and money.

Underestimated Potential

Are you realistic about your husband? When God shows you his ability along some line, do you encourage him with all your heart? Some husbands are the super-conscientious type who could really do several things well, but they are afraid to launch out for fear the undertaking will not be done "perfectly." A word of encouragement from a wife does wonders to build up a man's confidence and enables him to go ahead. Encouragement builds the confidence which leads to success. Every husband needs a cheering squad in his corner. Then remember to cheer when he does succeed!

There are times when a woman's pride holds her husband back and keeps him from doing what he ought to do, or what he would like to do. For example, some women discourage their husbands from teaching Sunday school. Some have even told the superintendent not to ask them to teach. Why? It's pride. Maybe they were afraid of losing face while he was learning to be at ease in front of people. If others appreciate your husband, why don't you?

Pride

Jean's fiancé loved to sing and people loved to hear him. However, she grew up believing that it wasn't right to sing before an audience unless you had a fully trained, concert voice. Ted invited her to go with him to a little church where he was asked to sing. He had sung there many times. The congregation loved to hear him for there was something about the *way* he sang that went straight to their hearts! Ted stood with quiet self-confidence. He had a lovely tenor voice, but, to Jean's

127

horror and humiliation, when he reached a high note in the chorus . . . he squeaked! And in front of all those people! And he was *her* fiancé! To think that anyone would get up and sing in public who *knew* he would squeak on a high note! Afterwards, with a few well-directed remarks, Jean squelched Ted's desire to sing in public. She never recognized his real gift to that small congregation, and completely missed the message which he sang so clearly. She never thought that the hymn could have been lowered to suit his voice, or that the people who asked him to sing liked to hear him, even if he didn't sing like Caruso. She saw nothing but her embarrassment. What if it weren't polished singing . . . what if it weren't perfect? Later God dealt with her attitude. She realized the selfishness of her foolish pride, but it was too late. She had killed something very precious in Ted. She had stifled something that could not be restored. What an unforgettable lesson.

Consequences of Undeveloped Gifts

In Matthew 25:14-30 we read the story of a rich landholder who gave his servants money to invest according to their abilities. To one servant he gave five talents, to another two talents, and to the third, one talent. The story goes on to tell how the first two men invested their money and doubled the original investment. The third man hid his money and, when the landlord returned, he gave him back exactly what he had been given in the first place. The master was angry with his lazy servant and commanded that the talent be taken from him and given to the first man. The lazy servant was cast into outer darkness.

How important it is that each person develop his God-given gifts. You must not ignore what you feel to be inferior talents. If you use your God-given gifts, He will develop them into something beyond what you have ever dreamed.

Nagging

A nagging wife will, in the end, tear down her husband inwardly. She'll only create resistance to her suggestions and *drain him of any desire to please her* and to do his work well. She may feel this is the way to help her husband be his best but unfortunately this backfires into resentment, discouragement and bitterness. But love and encouragement are tremendous incentives to your husband to be what you know he can be. Instead of settling for second best, a loving wife wants to do even better to prove her husband's faith was not misplaced. *In the warm climate of your understanding love he will be more free to find himself.*

Failure

A loving wife makes it safe for her husband to fail. God does not punish us for failure. He is there to support and encourage us to renewed effort. Can your husband feel your confidence in him while he is facing some problem, even though things do not come out as you expect? Even when he fails? Would he hesitate to tell you that he lost his temper on the job, and that it could ruin his reputation? Would he feel free to tell you of the threat of an employee cutback which could cause him to lose his job? Is he free to change jobs?

Experimenting

Lyn's husband, Paul, was an idealist. There were times when she felt some of his ideas were unrealistic. Things went well for a number of years. Then Paul felt he should change jobs. Lyn was afraid the new job would be totally unsuitable for him, but it was something he felt compelled to try. For the first time in their marriage they went into debt. As time dragged on Lyn became more and more nervous. She had confidence in her husband's abilities but she doubted the wisdom of the change. What if he failed? What should she do? What should be her attitude to Paul's new work, and how should she pray? Lyn felt confused in the pressure of trying to make ends meet.

However, an invitation to spend a few days away from home with her sister, enabled her to think objectively. During this time she was able to commit her fears and doubts to God. In this new inner freedom she expected God to show her husband the best way without her nagging or criticism. It was now safe for Paul to fail. It would not make *him* a failure in her eyes. When she returned home, she was able to share her ideas with Paul. Together they reevaluated Paul's abilities which eventually led him into more suitable work. In time, this difficult incident proved to be a rich experience for them. Not only did Paul find it was safe to fail, but this experience prepared him for his next occupation.

Chapter Eight
Problems Women Face

Questions to Ask Yourself

— What do you do with your problems?
— What can you do if you husband is away often?
— How should you cope with an interrupted schedule?
— Why is your husband job-hopping? What sort of job is best suited to his training, ability, temperament?
— What is your husband's realistic potential?
— How can you best encourage this in him?
— In what way does pride reveal itself in your life? What will you do about this?
— In what areas do you nag your husband? How can you encourage creatively instead of nagging destructively?

"Seek ye the kingdom of God; and all these things shall be added unto you. Fear not, little flock; for it is your Father's good pleasure to give you the kingdom" (Luke 12:31, 32).

9

Questions Women Ask

The former chapters discuss some everyday problems that wives encounter. Many of these can be solved when a woman's attitude is right toward God, herself, her husband and the problem. I trust that the illustrations and principles have crystalized vague thoughts and confirmed ideas about which you may have been uncertain. However, I feel the majority of questions that puzzle many married women are all a part of the challenge of merging together two personalities with their multitude of differences.

How I'd love to incorporate the scores of questions women have asked me over the years, but that would be impossible. The ones selected can only be representative. Since some questions need professional answers, I have not sought to deal with deep psychological problems or bizarre behavior patterns, but rather with everyday situations.

Many problems start small and develop into a totally unnecessary explosion. "Behold how great a matter a little fire kindleth" (James 3:5). Forest fires in the home can be prevented if you can detect the first flare of a struck match. It takes maturity to neither add fuel to the fire nor fan the flame of anger.

You can often find help from a friend in whom you have confidence, one who may not have all the answers, but who will be honest with you and with whom you can be honest.

Sharing your experiences and praying for God-given wisdom can throw light on your path and give you strength and courage.

Psychiatrists can help uncover hidden sins like bitterness, jealousy, hatred or insecurity, but *only God* can forgive these sins and provide the cleansing and healing which sets a person free to be himself — a channel of love.

Uncommunicative Husbands

How do you communicate with a man who won't talk? What are some of the reasons that would keep a man from talking?

There are at least three reasons why some men don't talk.

Some have never been talkers.

Some talk so much on the job that they want to be quiet when they are home.

Some have been deeply hurt so they have retreated into silence.

Into which category does your husband fall?

If your husband has never been a talker, why worry just because you love to talk. Look for the many ways a silent man can communicate: by touch, a look, thoughtful deeds, gifts or his contented presence at home. Allow him freedom to express his love in *his way*. Perhaps you could cultivate a common quiet interest like fishing or bowling. At least you'd be together. However, it doesn't hurt to say to him, in the right spirit, "It would mean so much to me if *just once* you'd say, I love you."

When you realize your husband is not talking because he does so much of it at work, then it becomes a privilege to provide as much quiet as possible for him at home. After your warm, welcoming embrace, your gift of silence will be refreshing to him. It probably won't be many hours before he's talking naturally and happily again.

If you recall happy times of communication in the early days of your marriage, ask God to help you to think back to *when* and if possible *how* the silence began. You may have to ask your husband how you hurt him. Did he feel belittled? Were his stories corrected, or expressions reworded? Maybe he was slow in expressing his thoughts and you were unaware of his feelings and used to rush in and finish his ideas for him. Or before he had time to finish you started on something else. Ask God to show you what caused the problem. If it has been going on a long while don't be discouraged if it takes time to undo the pattern of years.

Husbands in Good Light

How can I let the children see how wonderful their dad is? Outsiders think he is great but at home he is often irritable and short with them after a long and trying day at work.

Many times a wife can be a buffer for her husband. When you hear him cut off the children, you could say, "Look kids, your dad is tired now. Let him relax. Ask him after supper."

Ask God *how* and *when* to talk to your husband about the problem. Point out his wisdom and the children's need to see him at his best, like his friends do. Ask God how to communicate to your husband without making him feel accused or defensive. When you stay positive and your husband gets the message that you want his greatness to show to the children, you should be able to work out a way together in spite of your husband's pressures.

At meals it is easy to refer a difficult question that one of the children has posed to your husband. Or maybe you can introduce a meaningful subject with which your husband is conversant. In such a relaxed atmosphere, children can absorb a father's wisdom because their mother brought it into focus.

In-laws

My in-laws insist we spend every Sunday with them. With several children it is getting harder and harder to

133

go. What should we do? We don't want to hurt their feelings.

Ask God to prepare the hearts of your in-laws and trust that they'll understand. Lovingly explain to them how difficult a weekly visit is. Assure them of your love, but suggest visiting once a month, or during vacations. Or would it be easier if you suggested they come to you? Or perhaps some extra phone calls could bridge the gap of frequent visits.

I know of a man who wrote his in-laws a rather harsh letter declaring his and his wife's independence. The letter hurt (in his case understanding parents) but it set the young man free. Later he apologized for the tone of his letter and won the deep respect of his in-laws. This established a relationship with his in-laws on a mature, happy, adult level.

Possessive Mother

My mother calls me nearly every day. She tries to run our marriage and if we don't do what she says, she goes on and on calling me names and makes me feel awful. What can I do?

First God will have to set you free inwardly from your mother. Face your fear of her. Then when she calls, be polite, but firm. Thank her for calling, thank her for her interest and ask her to pray for you if that is fitting. Make no promises as you thank her for each suggestion. Tell her you have to go. Then hang up! Your mother will come to respect the evidence of your free adulthood.

This could happen overnight but such freedom usually takes time and practice.

Family Worship

Isn't it the husband's responsibility to conduct family worship?

It really doesn't matter who *conducts* family worship. The important thing is the spirit in which it is done. Due to the fact that the husband has so many other things on his mind it is sometimes easier for the wife to plan for this time. Perhaps the wife can read more easily than her husband, and it can save him embarrassment if she will do the reading. If he is free to pray let him take that part, or let the children take turns praying. Do the thing which makes the whole family feel the most comfortable.

If your husband does not profess to be a Christian or if he has some strong objection to family worship, could you find some time other than right after supper? Could you pray with the children when you tuck them into bed or at breakfast if your husband has already left for work? When there are a number of areas in which a husband and wife disagree it is a good principle to create as few issues as possible. This is, in part, what it means to adapt to your husband.

There are some women who seem to flaunt their faith, belittling their husband's lack of it. No wonder their husbands are not interested in Christ or family worship.

A man wants to see that his wife's faith works out in her home life, giving her patience with the children, loving acceptance of him, peace in trial and in many other practical areas of life and not just in a setting of religious ritual. He may not be interested in religion but he is vitally interested in reality. As he sees reality in the life of his wife he will be more interested in the means that brought it about.

Physical Hardship

"Do you think it is right to pray that my husband earn more? I get little for groceries and we have so little to live on and I can't give to the church or anything." (In this case even though her husband received a meager wage, she accepted her circumstances without complaint. However, a message she heard had awakened the thought that it might not be wrong to look to God for something better.)

There is nothing wrong with praying for more money. It is the *love* of money which is evil, not the desire to have an adequate provision for the family and a little extra to share with others. Many husbands do look for extra work which is a challenge and a complete change from their routine jobs. This could lessen the financial squeeze.

I know a man who, in addition to his regular job, helps people finish their basements or does odd jobs for a hobby. He enjoys working with his friends and, incidentally, earns a little more on the side to augment his rather slim income.

I have known of women who drive their husbands to overwork because of their greed. They long to keep up with the Joneses, or want to satisfy some whim. This is wrong!

Paul said, "I have learned, in whatsoever state I am, therewith to be content" (Philippians 4:19). Contentment is God-given but *complacency is sin*. What are your goals for your home? Is it large enough for your growing family? Is it suitable for entertaining your children's and husband's friends? Is it a place in which they enjoy gathering? Can you reorganize your home and make it do, or is it really inadequate for your family's needs? Ask your husband if more room would make your home a more relaxed place in which to live.

God has a way particularly adapted to *your* family's happiness. Ask Him to help you and your husband explore all the resources He has given you together. Then you can work out the way best suited to your family situation. You may even find that a hobby of yours could bring a little extra income and ease the family load.

Difficult-to-Live-With Husbands

Let me share excerpts from a letter containing the type of questions women often ask me.

Dear Jill,

I have often wished I could just sit and have a heart-to-heart talk with you. Instead I'll write. First of all, let me say how thankful I am for the

Winning Women Retreats. . . . There the Holy Spirit was able to complete a work in my heart that He tried to do at other times. It wasn't accomplished sooner because I couldn't see beyond my self-pity and hatred — yes, hatred — for my own Christian husband.

Oh, what a release from prison walls when I saw, confessed and put away my self-pity and hatred. I realized that my husband's way of life stemmed from his background which was far worse than mine. I began to do what would *help him personally* in our marriage relationship and in our home life. Once released from hatred and self-pity *things began to change*. I would love to tell you about this in detail, but it is more than I can write.

Jill, there are two questions that stand out in my mind. First, is it possible, in stressing the authority of the husband and the submission of the wife, that we are missing the boat as to what Christ *really* intends for a Christian relationship? I don't know if you are aware of the fact that there are many homes where parents and children are Bible-reading Christians and church attenders. The husband is deeply respected in the church but has an awful temper at home. His wife and children are fearful and the home is full of tension.

Do you know how many Christian homes are messed up by a wrong interpretation of husbands being the head of the home and wives submitting? I know of a woman who allows her husband to beat her and verbally abuse her because she feels this is submitting as Christ submitted to His abusers.

My second question is this: How can we as mothers whose husbands don't see as we see and feel as we feel about Christian standards raise our children wholesomely? Jill, there are not too many "ideal Christian homes." There are homes where the mother feels that certain TV programs are not healthy for growing minds and yet the father insists

137

on watching these programs himself. In other words, how can we help our families? Is it possible to teach our children to be "in the world, but not of the world"?

I don't know if I make sense to you at all, but these are the thoughts from my heart and I hope to find out how the Lord really feels concerning these things. By this I mean I am open to learning. I've come a long way since I've taken on an attitude of wanting to learn and *I've been freed from a rut!*

Thanks again . . .
Love,
Margaret

After reading Margaret's letter, I was reminded of a letter to Jane Lee from a lady who had discovered from her own experience how Jesus Christ can change an impossible marriage relationship.

Wife Thankful She Decided Not to End Unhappy Marriage

Dear Jane Lee: The two men who oppose divorce and remarriage quote the Bible in their letters and tell us, "What God has joined together, let no man put asunder," and that marriages are supposed to last "until death do us part."

But between the "I do" and "death" there is a heap of living to do. You don't quote two or three lines and then stand in judgment of those who get divorces. It goes deeper than that.

Own Experience

God didn't intend for us to marry and live a "living hell" on earth. He gave us words to guide, reproach, improve and comfort us along the way. I speak from experience. After eight years of a nightmare called marriage, I wanted to end it all, although I have two lovely children. Everything

I did was wrong, although I thought I was doing my best.

My husband was a bitter and angry man. He resented working and continually threatened to leave us so I went to the best marriage counselor, our Creator, God. From the time I accepted Christ as the One who bore all our sins, my past was automatically a closed door.

The shackles of bitterness, jealousy, self-pity and selfishness that bound my soul slowly disappeared and I was starting a new life with God as my guide.

With this second chance on life I explored the Bible and I discovered the way God, who loves us, wants us to live, if we choose.

Judge Not

He wants us to love (to care for all the needs of our husbands), to honor (to respect his thoughts and wishes and uphold whatever good we see in him), to obey, to be thankful in everything.

We are to be understanding, to judge not, to be prayerfully patient, merciful, pure in heart, peacemakers.

Husbands and wives are to love each other as they love themselves, striving to please each other.

We are to be respectful of others because we are not perfect. We are to forgive as we would like to be forgiven.

I have only scratched the surface, for each page of the Bible is a new adventure in learning.

I *didn't expect my husband to change* so I could in turn be a better wife, but *I chose to change* and after nine years my husband has changed despite himself. Now he is my constant, loving and dearest companion.

What I'm trying to say is that just telling someone he shouldn't divorce isn't enough.

A couple should be willing to work at marriage and want a better way of life. It's not the easy way but for me it is the most rewarding.

Her Way

When a relationship is what it should be no man can separate a man and his wife because their roots are deep and their foundation is built on truth.

Jane, perhaps you will choose not to print this letter as it really does sound old-fashioned and it might offend some people in our modern times. But this is the way I choose to walk and I do so with a spring in my step and a song in my heart.

God's Child

Jekyll-Hyde Husbands

Margaret, in her letter, referred to a type of professing, Bible-reading man who often appears to be a "saint" in public and "something else" at home. How does a wife live with this double standard of behavior so common today? How does a wife "adapt" to such a life, still keep her own sanity, and protect her children from psychological damage? I do not have the whole answer, but perhaps some suggestions could help lead toward an answer.

Women tend to accept their problems in one of two ways. They either talk a great deal about minor incidents, running down their husbands before their friends, or they keep quiet for years about his unchristian conduct at home thinking this is a part of submission — far worse, women think they have been taught that whatever happens is God's will; therefore they are to silently accept all abuse. They think this is the way to demonstrate true Christianity in the home. Some feel that since Christianity is *supposed* to give them a happy, victorious life, they're too proud to admit it isn't working for them as they imagine it must be working for others.

There is a *delicate balance* in true submission that is built on a *functioning faith*. Only the Holy Spirit can direct in each individual's case, as He did with "God's Child." Submission is the *God-given attitude which helps a woman to find the balance between being a door mat or a domineering shrew.* Husbands lose respect for a wife they can walk all over.

A friend of mine wrote out of the depths of her years of experience:

> "The Lord gave me boldness to do something about Frank instead of going along any longer . . . If I had stood up to Frank long ago *in the right way,* I'm convinced he'd never have gotten into the shape he did — not to *demand my rights* but to help him face what he was doing to himself and his family. But all I did was to criticize and thus put him on the defensive, rather than express *how* what he was doing affected me and leave the results with the Lord as I have now learned to do."

> Some time later my friend's husband wrote his father-in-law how grateful he was for such an encouraging wife.

There is a balance between being yourself and being a complete individualist running counter to others. God can show you how to have *your needs met* as an individual in your own right and still "adapt" to your husband. Such a relationship can draw out the best in each of you to strengthen your home and marriage.

On the other hand several wives have come to see how subconsciously they tormented their husbands. In a subtle way they drove them to their limit. (There is a time and a *way* to speak and a time and a *way* to keep silent. Some silence can be thunderous, threatening or disintegrating.) A wife can derive cruel satisfaction from seeing her husband lose control of himself, being literally driven to hit her. In this way she proves her superiority as he degrades himself by striking her.

However, there is nothing more thrilling when, by contrast, a wife sees how she can *channel her strength* behind her husband to help him become twice the man

141

he would have been without her individual gifts and character to supplement his abilities.

Wholesome Children

Now, to answer Margaret's question regarding raising children wholesomely in a home with differing standards. Actually she is well on the road to harmony in her home by her changed attitudes and her freedom from a judging spirit toward her husband. She has come to see, too, her need to *love* the children through their "ugly" periods.

It is so normal for children to play one parent against the other, but God will give you wisdom to handle this in your particular situation in some way which would be agreeable to you both. This can be done in a way to strengthen a father's role in the home. Really it is more important for children to *respect their father* than for them to be shielded from certain TV programs.

Take your problem of differences to God. It is of vital importance to keep the right attitude toward your husband and to present a united front to the children. Be careful not to communicate rejection of his person when you disagree with his way. At a "right" time and in a "right" spirit, discuss your differences with your husband privately. If you find yourself in sharp disagreement with him, ask him to explain his viewpoint. Let him know you appreciate his balance should you be too strict. Try to find the positive aspects of his ideas which you *can* support. Let him know you need his help with your emotional responses. Then you can turn your point of view over to God. Often, in the early years of our marriage, when there were differences of opinions in our home, I prayed:

"God, if *You* see this is really important, I expect You to show Fred. If not, set me free from my opinions and help me to accept Fred's way." There were times when Fred changed (though often he was unaware of it) but perhaps even more often *I* changed!

142

Trapped

How can I get away from this feeling of being trapped with little children and limited money?

Some wives may find it fun to exchange their children for a day with a friend. An occasional free day can release a homemaker and give her a whole new outlook on life. A day to rest or shop, have your hair done, take a class or visit a friend without taking the children, can restore your perspective and refresh you as a person. By afternoon you will be looking forward to returning to your home and children.

One wife wrote to me of how she had found a way to give enjoyment to her husband and a little free time for herself.

I became aware of my husband's sense of values and have been able to work out a way to meet my need for occasional freedom from the house and meals. Dale appreciates getting his money's worth. I looked around our area and found a place where, on certain days, you can eat all you want. There is another place where ample servings of good food make it a place worth visiting. Dale came to enjoy these outings too. An extra bonus is that we're able to teach our children good manners in public.

Gentlemanliness

"How did your husband become such a gentleman?" women have asked a friend of mine.

They wouldn't need to ask if they saw the glow in my friend's eyes and heard her enthusiastic appreciation for her husband's thoughtfulness. Women envy not only obvious courtesies but the extra little attentions of remembering dates or bringing flowers for no special reason. Some men are "naturally" more aware of these little deeds which mean so much to a woman. But it helps a lot to *start right*. For example, let your husband be the gentleman he'd like to be by opening the car door for you. Don't relax to the point of jumping out yourself.

143

In the daily routine of life it is easy to become careless. Husbands appreciate wives who encourage them to be gentlemen at all times. They like to be challenged to their best on every occasion, even though they may grumble a bit! Common courtesy then becomes a comfortable, happy way of life, not something put on when company comes.

Disagreement

How can I go along with my husband when I know he's wrong?

When there is a disagreement in policy between husband and wife, remember, God holds the husband responsible (Numbers 30:6-8). In normal instances the husband should have the final say and his word should be carried out. If the godly wife fears the wisdom of her husband's way, her recourse is (confident) prayer. How often I have seen God change a situation when a wife expressed clearly how she felt but *avoided making an issue of it*. She put her complete trust in God and He took care of the situation in His way.

But I've also seen the mess a family can get into when the wife takes things into her own hands. The ideal is to wait until you can both agree. Pray about the situation and be willing to do only what's best for the whole family. Does the issue *have* to be decided at once? Many wives were glad they waited for their "slower" husbands and accepted his judgment, because what had looked to the wife like an ideal prospect turned out to be a bad one.

Love for Hate

How can I love a man after I've lost all my love and respect for him?

Remember, a large part of love is a choice of the will. Choose to love your husband. Ask God for His gift of love. Thank God for giving it to you and then begin to act lovingly. God has commanded us to love one another for He Himself is love. As God lives in you

144

you can draw on His love through you to your husband. ". . . by prayer and supplication with thanksgiving let your requests be made known unto God" (Philippians 4:6). Our loving Father knows how easily we lose our perspective during conflict; thanking Him turns our eyes to His faithfulness and frees us to do what is right.

When love is fed it grows. As First Corinthians 13 puts it, love is unselfish, creative, patient and kind. It helps so much if you'll accept your husband as *he is,* not as you had hoped he would be.

As each annoyance comes up pray in your heart, "Thank You, Father, for Mike. I love him. Thank You that we can have a happy home. Set me free from making an issue and focusing on what is personally offensive to me . . . lateness . . . loudness . . . sloppy ways. Thank You for taking away my resentment." Then concentrate on a loving greeting when Mike is late. Hang up his coat, speak softly and remember all his fine qualities. You may not be able to change Mike but *you can* change your attitude toward your differences. In that way half your battle is won!

Too Tired to Love?

You will be amazed at what a fifteen minute rest in the afternoon can do for your attitude. A tired, dragged-out wife is no fair welcome for any husband. There are times when rest is impossible, but make it your aim, for your husband's happiness . . . and your own!

How Can I Cope With My Jealousy?

There are differences in the makeup of men and women that create misunderstandings and provoke jealousy. Women often do not understand what is behind a man's actions. They misread his natural conduct as lack of love or fidelity. Men are more aggressive and independent by nature — straining against things that bind and restrain them — even love. Often a wife feels threatened by her husband's struggle to keep free. She

145

feels he is trying to get away from *her,* that he no longer loves her. Could it be another woman? Jealousy wraps its tendrils around her heart and mind and fills her with fear and suspicion, which grows as imagined evidence is built on misinterpretation. Gradually her whole perspective becomes warped. A man doesn't stop to consider the basis for her fears. Instead he wonders what is wrong with his wife and is dismayed at her ridiculous lack of logic and common sense. Somewhere I read a good story which illustrates this feeling.

Nancy and Cliff were very much in love when they married and all went well for some months. Then Cliff came to Nancy with a blunt request. "Honey, there is one thing I feel I want in our marriage. I feel I have a right to have one night out a week with NO QUESTIONS ASKED."

Nancy was dumbfounded, but she had the wisdom to say nothing. She suffered with the implications of this request. When she could stand it no longer she went to her minister for advice.

"May I retaliate by having my night out with the girls, just to let him see how it feels?" she asked.

"I would suggest you let Cliff go. Refuse to allow suspicion to grow between you. Rather than going out alone, plan times when the two of you can do something special together," he suggested wisely.

It was not without a real struggle, but Nancy realized the wisdom of the advice. She gave Cliff a warm welcome when he returned home, asking no questions. She just chatted about her day or something interesting she had read. She planned things they could do together that they both could enjoy.

After a few weeks Cliff began to share with Nancy what he did on his "nights off." He went bowling with his friends or to the home of one of them for a bull session. He seemed less and less inclined to go out alone and in the weeks that followed, he stopped going altogether. Then one day he opened his heart. "Nancy, how can I thank you for your understanding and trust of me? When I was growing up my mother hounded me all the time. I couldn't do *one* thing without having to *report* to her. I hated it and wasn't going to have this in my marriage too." Nancy was amazed. Little did she realize that Cliff's attitude to his *mother* could have ruined their marriage.

Men are less inhibited than women, and often a woman will interpret his natural outgoingness as an inclination to stray. She needs to be less judgmental until she comes to understand how her husband's love for her is expressed differently. Men have a different language to express their inmost feelings, a "language" reserved for their wives. Wives need to learn to recognize this.

It is built into men to be interested in women. They *are* subject to temptation by other women. Many times, much to a wife's dismay, men enjoy flirting with this temptation. "He doesn't really love me," the wife will say. "He just wants me to be his maid, and see that his house and children are cared for and his clothes washed and ironed." But this is usually the farthest thing from a husband's mind. If he enjoys playing with fire, don't waste your time in jealous, resentful thoughts.

Women need to build the best defense they can to help their husbands against temptation. *Make it your aim to see that his deep emotional needs are completely satisfied at home — by you.* Be attractive, loving, stimulating, full of fun and encouragement. Be sure he knows he is important in his home and in your life. Be sure his need for sex is met by a loving wife who finds a real thrill and enjoyment in sharing his love. This will become his best defense and yours.

But what if he has yielded to temptation? What if your jealousy is well-founded? What then? Your heart rebels, you want to retaliate, to reject him as he has rejected you. You don't see any way to go on. . . .

147

You might as well separate, you think. But is this the way of love? Is this God's way? He says to forgive as He has forgiven. You say your love has died. Then ask God to renew it, to overrule the hurt and humiliation. This will take a miracle, but pray that God will give you the *right attitude*.

Now *look to yourself*. With God's help, begin to remake yourself, your spirit, your mind, and your looks. Read Philippians 4:8: "In conclusion, my brothers, fill your minds with those things that are good and deserve praise: things that are true, noble, right, pure, lovely, and honorable" (*Good News for Modern Man*). Make these thoughts the basis of your thinking and conversation. Read Galatians 5:22 and 23: "But the Spirit produces love, joy, peace, patience, kindness, goodness, faithfulness, humility, and self-control. There is no law against such things as these" (*Good News for Modern Man*). Let this be the attitude of your heart. Ask God to make you altogether lovely, and free from any bitterness, self-pity and resentment.

Then rebuild your life. Find some satisfying, recreating activity to rebuild your self-esteem, enrich your life, stimulate you mentally, and enable you to grow as a person. Keep your home, your children and your husband's things in order and up-to-date, and maintain your own self-respect. Turn your husband over to God. You can trust Him to take care of you both. Let your heart be at peace . . . the peace which only God can give when your situation calls for anything but peace . . . a complete confidence in God, that leaves you free to be all God intended you to be, regardless of your husband's behavior.

His Jealousy

Some women are tormented by jealousy — not theirs, but their husband's. You haven't done a thing wrong, yet he is constantly suspicious of your every move.

148

There is nothing you can do, nowhere you can go but what he objects or suspects or even forbids. You might just as well be in jail. In your effort to placate him you give up all your activities one by one. Then you give up your friends, and sometimes even your family. But that doesn't help either. Or maybe you are more rebellious and you say: "Well, there's no pleasing him anyway. I'll live my own life and he can go hang. It's none of his business what I do, since he won't believe me anyway." This is one of the hardest attitudes for a wife to overcome. What is she to do to please her husband and prove to him she *is* a good trustworthy wife? Many times the only answer lies with God. Put the whole thing before Him, and ask Him to *show you the key to your husband's fear*. It may take a long time, plus much patient understanding on your part. But think of the longsuffering of God toward you before you came to trust Him. Keep on showing your love in a sweet, uncritical spirit. Do the things that are right. Live a normal life with your children, friends, family, and outside activities, but be sure these do not cut in on your time with your husband. Make your times with him rich and enjoyable so that he knows you love to be with him and to share his enjoyment.

Be completely trustworthy — avoid any appearance of evil. Resist the urge to show your husband up as a jealous-without-cause brute. Be open with him, not only answering all his spoken and unspoken questions, but volunteering things you think he would want to know, or that might make him suspect that you are concealing things from him. Then *be very patient with the fear* that is behind his jealousy. Give your love consistently without reaction or retaliation, openly and freely no matter what he says or does. Try to help him see through your own conduct and his experience with you that he has nothing to fear; that he will not lose you nor your love. This is a big test and a big hurdle

149

for him. God who made him will have to reveal to you how to show the love that your husband will recognize as safe, stable, genuine and trustworthy. Then he can relax.

A friend of mine told me of her husband's jealousy when they were first married. He had grown up in a home of suspicion and jealousy, some of which was well grounded. These attitudes had been absorbed by the sons. This young wife was able to see the basis for her husband's feeling by talking things over. She developed a good relationship and in time the husband was wonderfully freed from his jealousy.

How Do I Resist Temptation?

What should you do when you are tempted — or even fall — into adultery? Perhaps you are feeling deeply unsatisfied or even revengeful. At such times a wife can be tempted, either by an intense sexual affinity or because of her own emotional hungers.

Recently a woman told me of her agony and fear because she was so strongly drawn to a man in her church. She could see he felt much the same way. She knew well the sin of such lust: ". . . anyone who looks at a woman (man) and wants to possess her (him) is guilty of committing adultery with her (him) in his (her) heart" (Matthew 5:28, *Good News for Modern Man*). After days of battling within herself (while staying clear of the man), she finally confessed her sin and was willing to have God remove this feeling. He did. The power of this affinity was broken and the wife turned to pour out understanding love to her own husband with whom she had little in common.

Few women have time to be involved in extra-marital affairs when concentrating on creative homemaking and seeking the best for their husbands and going one hundred percent of the way in giving love. Fifty-fifty giving will never work, for who is to determine when fifty percent giving has been reached? Suppose he only gives forty-five percent? Then what? One hundred percent giving needs to be a settled life principle, for only then will giving-love reach across the chasm of need to the heart of the other.

How Can I Handle My Moods?

Most women I've talked to have this problem, but few realize how many people are affected by their moods nor do they know how to cope with them. Moods are due to changes in a woman's body chemistry which cause her nerves to be frayed at times. It has only been in recent years that much has been written on the subject. When you suddenly feel crabby and the world is against you, check the calendar! These moods come in cycles about once a month usually before the menstrual period. A woman can gain as much as five to seven pounds during this period of hormone change. She becomes tense and irritable. What she could take in her stride yesterday, she feels unable to cope with today. Usually after menstruation a woman's feelings are relieved and she returns to normal. But your question is: "How can I live with myself and others during moods and depression."

Your recognition that this pre-menstrual tension is *physical* can solve half your problem. Then you can make provisions ahead if at all possible to avoid pressure and strain while your body is in this state. This can help smooth your feelings and keep you from blaming your husband for this "sudden" lack of consideration and the children for being more unreasonable than usual!

Accept the situation as *normal and deliberately relax.* When the cloud descends on you, see if you can find a quiet place for a few minutes. Then turn your body over to your Maker . . . God knows your frame . . . (Psalm 103:14). He who has made you understands

151

your physical tensions. Ask Him who made your body to undertake for you with one of His miracles. Ask Him to release the tension and give you the inner composure you need — right now. Thank Him. Then go about your work in the confident joy and release of answered prayer. You will be amazed at the results. Later as you look back over your day, you will marvel at the way you were able to live through it. This is not theory. I can't tell you the number of times, when I have been either cross or overwhelmed with my load, I asked God then and there to help me and He did. He helped me to work *above* my feelings and not collapse *under* them.

How Can I Face Menopause?

The menopause seems to be a prolongation of pre-menstrual tensions! So, generally speaking, if you have been able to weather pre-menstrual tension nicely you should be able to breeze through this time of life. Really it is just as normal to leave the reproductive cycle as it was to come into it. We should be able to do it a bit more gracefully because we have matured emotionally since we were twelve or fourteen! However, there is a vast difference in the make-up of women, and if you need help through medication you should go to your doctor and tell him frankly of your need.

A woman doctor who wrote on this subject suggests you lighten your load during this time and take more time to rest. She feels more rest and less tension are helpful. As a doctor she understands the pressures of a busy life. If you are carrying a very heavy load, you should pray about delegating or dropping some of your work.

For other women their load is generally lighter during this time. Usually the children are in school and some of them have even left home. Some women have not yet found a creative and satisfying outlet. With less to do, the aches and pains and sleeplessness are accentuated. It would be better for you to have more to do. Ask your pastor or look around for a need you can fill. There are babies who need love or teens who need an understanding home. Overloaded pastors need help with typing and other jobs. Sick people and shut-ins need to be visited. There are hundreds of people who need prayer and an equal number who long for letters. Mission offices are usually understaffed; hospitals, convalescent homes and working mothers need volunteer help.

Ask God to show you where you are needed and for what worthwhile work He has prepared you and given you this new freedom — freedom for the richest phase of life with your husband. . . . "The best is yet to be. The last of life for which the first was made" (Browning).

Dread of Growing Old

Fears come with the changes in life — fear of declining attractiveness, old age, illness and other things. It is often easy to let down when you are older. Daughters are a good check here, and it is good to heed their advice about your appearance as they seek to put mother's foot forward!

You can't stop the passage of time but you can have a positive *attitude* toward it. Accept what you cannot change. Old age is beautiful when there develops with it an attending spirit of gentleness and forbearance. For one of my friends, life really began after fifty-five. Through her work and vision many are now kept busy providing homes for missionaries on furlough and caring for a retirement home. With purpose and vision come good health and vitality. Many women are "late bloomers" who find themselves later in life as they give themselves to others. As a woman accepts graciously the challenge of the passing years she will have more and more to contribute to her husband and grown family.

153

Overcoming Failure

There are times when each of us feels like a miserable failure in our marriage. Perhaps it is just that time of the month for you or perhaps you have said or done something which was not the wisest thing. But there is no need to grovel in the dust. All of us make mistakes. — we're human! But we don't have to stay "human." Talk to your heavenly Father. Tell Him all about the failure. Who but God can take away the personal humiliation and the feeling of being a failure as a wife. Ask Him for the remedy and then listen for His guidance. Admit *your* mistake; remedy it as far as you can and leave the rest to God. Just as many a loving parent untangles the messes his children get into, God will work out for you the "all things that work together for good" (Romans 8:28).

Proverbs 24:16 has been a bulwark of encouragement to me. "A righteous man (woman) falleth seven times," but what does she do? She falls seven times, but she "riseth up again." She does not stay down. She puts her hand in God's, gets up, and goes on with His help.

You have all the help you need for the glorious task of becoming a wonderful wife to have . . . and to hold! It will not come overnight, but it will come as you set your goal and work to that end. After years of marriage, you will look back on a life of deep satisfying fulfillment and joy in the task of making your loved one happy.

Handling Problems

Here are a few suggestions for facing realistically what you find difficult in your husband and home situation. It becomes exciting to see how God will lead you to find creative answers for problems, rather than being overwhelmed by the destructive despair that seizes so many wives. Take a sheet of paper and make two lists under the following headings:

Things in Him I Find a Problem	Things in Me He Finds a Problem
Temper	Too easy-going
His family	My mother
His TV viewing	Gabbing with friends
No communication	Spending too much money
Harsh way of talking	Too much worry and fussing
Different standards (list in detail)	Too legalistic
Indifferent to my needs (list each)	Habitually late

As you think through and meditate on these differences, ask yourself these questions.

1. Have I accepted my husband as he *is,* not as I hope he will be? You want him to accept *you.* First you must accept yourself for self-acceptance is a key to accepting the differences in others. This does not mean you do not look for a change, but it does mean that you are facing realistically the actual facts that are giving you a difficult time in your marriage.

   This first step is something few women can do just by deciding to do it. You need to *ask* and *expect* God to work a miracle. He will enable you to accept your husband — as is. He has promised, "Ask and ye shall receive, that your joy may be full" (John 16:24).

2. Have I truly forgiven my husband for the things he has said and done that have hurt me deeply?

   God's love does not keep a score card. As Jesus said to Peter, "You are to forgive seventy times seven" (Matthew 18:22). In other words, lose track of the number. In the thirteenth chapter of 1 Corinthians, Paul writes of the kind of love we should have. It suffers long and is kind (while it suffers)! Our Lord's Prayer tells us very simply that God will "Forgive us our debts *as we forgive* our debtors" (Matthew 6:12).

Look at your list again. You may have to change things or add to it. *Choose* to forgive him, regardless of how you feel . . . forgive him for losing his temper with you. Forgive him for each offense. (Never mind *his* wrong. He stands before God on that — you are *only* to take care of your attitude.) Deliberately forgive him

- for being unjust to one of the children
  - for not telling you he was working late at the office
    - for belittling you before your friends
      - for criticizing your housekeeping
        - for wasting money
          - etc.

3. Have I asked God's forgiveness for my bitterness . . . my anger? Have you let the sun go down on your wrath, when God has said, "Let not" (Ephesians 4:26)?

4. Have I *accepted God's forgiveness* and cleansing and *thanked Him* for it?

5. Have I accepted God's love for my husband? Live by the *fact* of that love and *not the feeling* which may not come until after you have begun demonstrating your love. In other words:

- Seek to understand your husband from *his* viewpoint.
  - Seek to please him (in meals, homemaking, the way you dress).
    - Encourage him and build him up.
      - With God's help through prayer develop a meek (great strength under control) and quiet (not mousy or suppressed) spirit.

156

6. Do I expect a change?

"Trust in the Lord, and do good . . . Delight thyself also in the Lord; and *he shall give thee the desires of thine heart.* Commit thy way unto the Lord; trust also in him; and he shall bring it to pass. . . . Rest . . . and wait patiently. . . . Cease from anger . . . fret not thyself . . ." (Psalm 37: 3-8).

Summary: What Do You Want and What Do You Expect?

Write down exactly what you want God to do for you. Remember, it is no disgrace to have a problem. We all have them. You have only to obey God and then watch expectantly while He does His work. Remember, "His ways are not our ways . . ." (Isaiah 55:8). His *methods* may surprise you, but you can have complete confidence in Him. Let down your heart. "Ask and ye *shall* receive, that your joy may be full" (John 16:24). Rest expectantly in His perfect love for you and His goodness toward you.

In time and perhaps even now your husband will look back over the years and see in you the wife "whose price is far above rubies."

"There are many fine women in the world, but you are the best of them all. Charm can be deceptive and beauty doesn't last, but a woman who fears and reverences God shall be greatly praised" (*Living Proverbs* 31:29, 30).

RECOMMENDED READING

PART I

Andelin, Helen B., *Fascinating Womanhood*. Santa Barbara, California: Pacific Press, 1965.
> The how-to of being a fascinating wife and drawing the highest and best out of a husband.

Carnegie, Mrs. Dale, *How to Help Your Husband Get Ahead*. New York: Pyramid Publications, Inc., 1957.
> Practical insights from the wife of an outstanding man.

Lees, Hannah, *Help Your Husband Stay Alive*. New York: Collier Books, 1962.
> How to do exactly that!

Miles, Herbert J., *Sexual Happiness in Marriage*. Grand Rapids, Michigan: Zondervan Publishing House, 1967.
> Excellent book on helping couples make adequate sexual adjustments. Explained in a wholesome Christian context.

Mow, Anna B., *The Secret of Married Love: A Christian Approach*. Philadelphia and New York: J. B. Lippincott Co., 1970.
> Author deals with and makes excellent suggestions for meeting the problems that arise in marriage.

Nichols, Ralph G. and Stevens, Leonard A., *Are You Listening?* New York: McGraw-Hill Book Co., Inc., 1957.
> Vital importance of listening and how to train oneself in the art.

Osborne, Cecil, *The Art of Understanding Your Mate*. Grand Rapids, Michigan: Zondervan Publishing House, 1970.
> Understanding helps to solve a lot of misunderstanding.

Robinson, Dr. Marie N., *The Power of Sexual Surrender*. Garden City, New York: Doubleday and Co., 1959
  Unusual help on melting frigidity and understanding the husband's as well as the wife's role.

Thieme, R. B., Jr., *The Biblical View of Sex, Love and Marriage*. Houston, Texas: Berachah Church.
  Author known for his biblical-based subject matter.

Tournier, Paul, *To Understand Each Other*. Richmond, Virginia: John Knox Press, 1967.
  The importance and suggested ways to achieve understanding of each other.

PART II

Better Homes and Gardens Editors, *Meals in Minutes*. Des Moines, Iowa: Meredith Press, 1963.
  One hundred eighty quickie recipes with illustrations.

Bracken, Peg, *The I Hate to Housekeep Book*. New York: Harcourt, Brace & World, Inc., 1962.
  Hundreds of delightful, humorous suggestions for streamlining and enjoying housekeeping and economizing.

Christenson, Larry, *The Christian Family*. Minneapolis, Minnesota: Bethany Fellowship, Inc., 1970.
  All the basics for successful family living today.

Gilbreth, Lillian M., et al., *Management in the Home*. New York: Dodd, Mead and Co., 1959.
  Excellent details from efficient kitchen arrangement to organizing your time by a real efficiency expert.

Hunt, Gladys, *Honey for a Child's Heart*. Grand Rapids, Michigan: Zondervan Publishing House, 1969.
  Makes the importance and choice of books in any family a must. Gives a wide scope of books to choose from for happiness and high ideals.

Miller, Ella May, *A Woman in Her Home*. Chicago, Illinois: Moody Press, 1968.
  The happiness and creative joy it can be.

Mow, Dr. Anna B., *Your Child*. Grand Rapids, Michigan: Zondervan Publishing House, 1963
Understanding and training your children in Christian character.

Mow, Dr. Anna B., *Your Teen-ager and You*. Grand Rapids, Michigan: Zondervan Publishing House, 1967.
Communicating love and probing problems between teens and parents.

Osborne, Cecil, *The Art of Understanding Yourself*. Grand Rapids, Michigan: Zondervan Publishing House, 1968.
Opens up a new world of yourself to yourself with understanding of how to solve problems.

Whiston, Lionel, *Are You Fun to Live With?* Waco, Texas: Word Books, 1968.
Showing how deeply God can change you.

Wonderly, Gustava M., *Training Children*. Chicago, Illinois: Moody Press, 1959.
Excellent detailed account of how to train a child for God from babyhood.

Zavin, Theodora and Stuart, Freda, *The Working Wives Cook Book*. New York: Crown Publishers.
Preparation timing and what can be done the night before.

PART III

Doty, Guy, *Divorce and Remarriage*. Minneapolis, Minnesota: Bethany Fellowship, Inc.
Scriptural basis for a deep study on the subject.

Ginott, Dr. Haim G., *Between Parent and Child*. New York: The Macmillan Co., 1965.
Practical advice and stories to help parents understand and train their children.

Rinker, Rosalind, *Prayer — Conversing With God*. Grand Rapids, Michigan: Zondervan Publishing House, 1959.
Practical way of conversing with God.